Buyers vs. Liars

Buyers vs. Liars

Secrets of the Auto Dealerships

INVEST IN THE WORLD'S GREATEST VEHICLE BUYING GUIDE

$aving Money is What It's All About

Don't Get Ripped Off Anymore by Dealerships

FIGHT FOR THE PRICE

**This Buyers' Payment Schedule Chart and Information Guidebook
Is for Automobiles, Trucks, Motorcycles, RVs, Boats, Jet Skis, etc.**

Darmonica G. Alexander

www.buyersvsliars.com

To order additional copies of this book, contact:
Xlibris Corporation
1-888-795-4274
www.Xlibris.com
Orders@Xlibris.com
54739

www.buyersvsliars@Xlibris.com
Email:buyersvsliars@yahoo.com

Contents

Dedication

I dedicate this book to my mother, Mary Alexander. She always told me to keep doing the right thing in life. This is also a special dedication to my son, Jason; my grandson, Jake; and Jake's mom, Jasmine Saunders.

Preface

AFTER YEARS OF working in the automobile business, I finally decided to write a book about my experiences. I started working at a Chrysler dealership in Carson, Calif., in September 1987. This job brought me much hard-earned commission. I was Salesman of the Month during my first month in the business and Salesman of the Year in December. I began to prepare this book and information guide as a salesman in 1989. I remembered a salesman named J.R. at the Chrysler dealership telling me, "Hey, little buddy, you know more about the car business than you think, but you're just too young to know it." He also said, "Don't stay at one dealership too long. You need to move around and sell different cars. You're sharp." This advice stuck in my mind and was the key to my success!

Being in Southern California and before working in the automobile business I wanted to hang out in Los Angeles, Beverly Hill and in Hollywood to meet some famous stars. That didn't happen, I managed to visit Disneyland, Beverly Hills (the Beverly Hills Hotel), Universal Studios (which is my favorite) and I did managed to get on the Dating Game Show" in 1988. There were 48 or more contestants trying to get on the show and the contestants were very serious about getting on the show, but I just wanted to go on a date and have some fun! After going through all of the preliminaries for one of their upcoming shows, I was actually called to be one of the three bachelors. They asked several hilarious questions, they asked the bachelorette who will be the lucky bachelor? She hesitated and said, "I choose bachelor number 2," and that was me. At first I wasn't too excited until the announcer told us "to pack our bags because we are going a 7 day adventurous to London, England with all bill paid,' then I got excited. At that time my five year old son (Jason) was in the audience cheering for me. We stayed at the Tar Hotel and attended a play the first night in London. We also visited "The Tower" where they kept some of their most precious diamonds. We shopped at Harold's (I could afford only some gloves) and then we partied at the Hippodrome Night Club. Wow what a game show! I had the time of my life.

Now as I continue to work in the automobile industry I began to realize that the automobile demand a lot of hours. Therefore I decide to get out of the automobile business all together. After working a few hourly jobs, there was no comparing in the hourly rates to the automobile's commission plan. So I rushed back into car sales so fast that no one knew that that I left. I also realized that it cost a lot of money to live in California period.

In 1990 I decide to relocate back to Northern California (the Bay Area). I proceeded to work in sales at Hill Top Ford and Bill Nelson Chevrolet but one my friend Marcus wanted to purchase a Jeep Grand Cherokee for his mother. Another friend wanted to purchase a Jeep from me for an upcoming ski trip at Lake Tahoe. I was hired at Smith Jeep dealership in Richmond, Ca. Now they had a "Demo Program," this is where the dealership's program that provided each salesman with a Jeep to drive. The salesman demo must be sold by him or another salesman with less than 8,000 miles in order to obtain another demo. The last year at Smith Jeep I attended the San Francisco Auto Show and representing Smith Jeep. After the Auto Show was over that weekend the owner's son Greg Smith told me that I won the Mystery Shoppers Award. I asked him what's a Mystery Shopper's Award? As I proceed into the business office, someone said, "Congratulation" you've won Jeep's Mystery Shoppers Award and here is a check for $250.00 and a free bed and breakfast weekend from the Marriott Hotel. The Mystery Shoppers award is where someone who pretends to be just a customer asking various questions for the sharpest person there who knows the manufacturers product of that certain models.

Another memorable moment at Smith Jeep was when my roommate/best friend "Pooe" (Hinton Box) wanted to buy a WV Jetta on our used car lot. But there were two Jettas on the lot. The Jetta with no power windows and no power locks was the advertised vehicle and the Jetta with power windows and door locks we switched the sale price. We took the Jetta out for a test drive as we had lunch and smoked some fat taylors and gave that Jetta a "new new car smell." I wrote the deal up and took it to my boss Bud Norris. He realized that I switched the vehicle's sticker price on the Jetta and he told me, "I going to fix your black ass for changing the sell price with a smile." This is what he did! Now Bud knew that I was a Dallas Cowboy fan and he was a San Francisco 49ers fan with season tickets. He said, "remember when you switched stickers on that Jetta for your buddy, well I taking you to see the NFC Championship Play-Off Game at Candle Stick Park between 49ers and the Cowboys, yea we are going to kick your butts, yea!" Well it back fired because the Cowboys kicked their butts and won that game. Bud and his wife took me out for dinner after the game. That year the Dallas Cowboys played the Buffalo Bills in Pasadena, Ca for the Super Bowl and won 52 to 17. I went to the Super Bowl in my Jeep demo. It broke down on me on the way back from the Super Bowl where it caused me $750.00 for the tow!

After working for Smith Jeep for three years, I decided to get into sales for Mitsubishis and my roommate's father Mr. Box purchased three vehicles from me. My roommate was my best customer! Now years earlier I was praying to God asking Him to bless me in writing my book and the next thing I heard a voice saying, "you haven't read my book." Therefore I began reading God's book. "In the beginning God created the heaven and the earth, and etc." My book Buyers vs. Liars was put on the shelf for years as I continued to read God's book and gather more experience in the automobile business. The next dealership was Hayward Ford, and they had too many different models in their inventor for me. This was too many product knowledge tests that were required and it took too much time studying and I just wanted to sell about 10-15, make $7,000.00 a month and take a vacations. This was too must for me and I was out of there!

Next I worked for Honda of Oakland and later I went to Hayward Honda in Hayward, Ca. Selling Hondas was very simple. There was two main vehicles to sell a "Honda Civic or a Honda Accord," simple! Of course they just the right amount of models to sell. Customers were very satisfied with their Honda vehicles and they would always send me referrals. After 12 years of sales, I was rightfully promoted to finance, special finance and assistance sales manager and knew the business pretty well. At that time our Manager was Jerry Fernandez and Bob Gee who promoted employees according to your skills. They voted me as the store MVP (Most Valuable Person) because I could sales, finance, and I had a 97% customer satisfaction with Honda. This became a good and a bad situation for me. What I mean about a good situation, because I always setting appointments with referred customers. The bad situation was that I rarely had any time for myself. The auto dealers demand twelve hours and more hours to where you might not have a good relationship at home.

Mean while Sonic Automotive a large dealership group who bought out the rights Hayward Honda. The new company Sonic, had a very powerful team with Jerry Fernandez and Bob Gee, they were professional and the dealership was in the right location. jerry and Bob left the dealership because they wanted to to cut their pay plan. Those jobs management positions were open and one day I would become General Manager.

One of the highlights of my life came when I was promoted from sales to the finance department. This move opened my eyes to even more money without standing outside and waiting on customers. The sales manager told me that the dealership's profit increased in every product from warranties, paint and fabric protection, and even from GAP insurance.

The sales manager asked me if I was interested in being a closer, because two of the assistant sales managers got into a physical altercation at work and were both suspended. I agreed to be the closer for both teams, meaning I would not have a day off for two weeks. To his amazement, my closing ability was higher than both closers combined.

My closing skills put more money in each salesman's pocket. One salesman named Abby was making only $100 commission whenever he sold a Honda Civic. I closed one of his deals on a Civic and earned him $700–on just one deal! Boy, did this 18-year-old go crazy. Abby bought me a chicken lunch every day, it was chicken this and chicken that, see Abby was from India and they don't eat any beef. I appreciated Abby and was very thankful him!

The next month, Abby earned $7,200 in commission with me as his closer. I was the top closer and earned the dealership nearly $100,000 that month.

My career came to an end when a new general manager came in and took away my Most Valuable Person (MVP) status. He also didn't want me to keep helping the new finance managers with some of their deals. At this time, a lot of contracts were being written incorrectly, and the bank was rejecting them. One weekend, the finance department was backed up with customers eager to get home. The new manager didn't want me to help her, because if I did the deals in the finance department, then I would earn that commission as finance manager as well as a closer. Once the manager saw the $6,000.00 front-end profit from the customer, he had no choice but to send me to do the finance paperwork. Once the paperwork was completed, I noticed the other manager was still struggling to close that same customer.

I brought my own customers to the dealership and sold them a vehicle and financed their contract paperwork. I could not understand why the GM was so upset with me. I was earning my commission. The more commission I earned, the more his paycheck would be.

Then Sept. 11, 2001, came and brought about a big change in my life and the lives of all Americans. Among other things, automobile industry sales declined. So I decided not to get back into this business. In 2001 Sonic Automotive hired a new General Manager by the name Ken Brizendine who thought that he was "god." He wanted to increase vehicle sales at this dealership after the incident of 911. I asked him if he could place me and the other closer Clay into the newspaper for advertising. He told me that if he placed our advertising in the newspaper that we would pay for it out of our own pockets. I looked at him as he was crazy, and he was. I didn't hear from him regarding advertising for a while. Weeks later Ken took my MVP status from me and gave it to my salesman Tom Chong. Next Ken had his friend Steve Chang to move from Southern California to Northern California for a job opportunity in sales. His plan was to turn Steve into something that he wasn't "a manager" over night. First he placed Steve on my team for two weeks and allowed him to create a new team at the same time. Then he took my "salesman of the month" (Tom) from my team and placed him on Steve's team. After hiring Steve he allowed him to interview sales consultants for his sales crew. Early one morning I heard the voice of God, said, get up, I don't like what they are doing to you, get up and gather your documents," that He did not like how they were treating me and to gather all of my documents from that dealership. I obeyed that voice and got to work early and gathered my documents. That same day while standing at the water fountain drinking water, that same voice said, "go outside" I'm a manager and I rarely goes outside. But I did what I was told and in about two minutes later a van pulled up passed all of the salesmen and they pulled up to me and they asked for Jenny. I asked them, "how did you hear about Jenny?" They showed me the Sing Tao Newspaper ad with Jenny and another sales consultant on the advertising with their cell phone number on the advertising. These two new hired sales consultants were placed in the newspaper the very first day of employment. The next day another sales consultant called and she said, "Darmonica, how did Steve and Tom get an ad in the newspaper and you did? I said, where? She said, "look in the Korean Times Newspaper." As I looked in the newspaper there it was Steve and Tom was also placed newspaper there it was, Now Steve was advertised as the sales manager as the sales manager (a title above me). This made me angry and upset! Now if that wasn't bad enough, Ken changed our full-time schedule to part- time schedules that gave Steve's team the advantage of setting appointment and earning more commission. I've never worked a 34 hours week ever in the car business and this was a first. This was clearly a violation of several of Sonic Automotive Company Policies. Remember, I asked Ken to place me in the newspaper ads before Steve relocated to the Bay Area. Ken's question to me how many languages do you speak? When he asked me that question I just walked away from him. I have heard that **"if you don't stand for something, then they will fall for anything."** I felt that Ken had discrimination against me. Ken was signing our checks averaging over $8,000.00 per month and he wanted his friend with no experience to do the same. Therefore I stood up for myself! As I did I heard the voice telling me to stand up for righteousness and I did. So I searched for an Attorney and God said, "you will go to court," "no you will to court and represent this case yourself." I said, "no way" and I continued attempted to search for an Attorney." God blocked all avenues! I attempted several times to hire an Attorney on my own and on the Internet. At first I didn't understand that I would personally take them to court. There is a saying that **"They say that a man who represents himself has a fool for a client and a fool for a lawyer."** Once I thought that I had an Attorney until I told them that the defendant was Sonic Automotive, they replied "we don't go against them." After reading God's words in His book, you must obey His voice.

So I did and found myself in court filing briefs and **amending** my case as if I was an Attorney. Once the trial finally got started and got near the end, Sonics Automotive Attorney told me that my case was filed Dec. 16, 2003 and that made it an untimely file case. The Judge ordered me to get him the correct papers showing that I my case was timely filed. Therefore I went back to the EEOC (Equal Employment Opportunity Commission) in Oakland, CA where my case was filed. When I got there one of the EEOC Agent's told me when I first file my case against Sonics Automotive, their Attorneys came down to review my file folder. As I made a request to see my file another Agents came out and told me that my file has been **"destroyed."** This is what God was trying to show me. He wanted me to see this for myself first hand and not from an Attorney's mouth. I had a great case and they knew it. I believe that the EEOC was paid off by Sonic Automotive Auto Group. The EEOC didn't know that I had a copy that was faxed draft copy by the EEOC Agent signed June 25, 2002 and not December 16, 2003 a year later. The EEOC played a very big part of me not win my law sue. The EEOC covered it up by giving me a letter stating that my case was timely file and I guess you can say that "big money took little money!'

The case ended in 2007 where I had lost the case and began to move on in my life. After humbling myself and obeying the Lord's voice, I received great jobs and wondered what happened. At that time I just thankful that the case finally was over, and again I was graceful.

Now years later in 2008 I heard the voice God again saying, "now get your book out and finish writing." Then God do good thing for my book! I wanted to purchase a $6,000.00 package from the publisher and I didn't have the money. I was able to purchase that package for $3,000.00 less. Therefore I continue to seek God first. He began blessing me in so many ways. While writing my book one day the evening news was on, as I looked over my shoulder and saw many dealerships all across America were closing down, and this accrued for several months. This economy was turning up side down and the auto dealer and the real estate market was hit the hardest. Some dealerships had to apply for a Government Bailout. "You reap what you sow."

Believe it or not there are still dealerships lying to customer harder, because business is slower. God played a very big part in this book and He must be recognized. Please stop and take the time out to read what God's word says about liars. Proverb 26: 23-28 and Proverb 6: 16-197 and that will sum it all up,

"God hates a liar!"

Now Buyers vs. Liars should open up many consumer eyes on how to protect themselves when purchasing a vehicle. And those unethical dealers out there, you are what you are.

Consumers with Poor Credit beware of dealerships who are telling customers that they must sent their contract to Nevada to get approved for 32% rates due to their poor credit score, instead of the 19% or 21% rates that they are charging. These dealerships need to be investigated. This is a violation against the **Truth in Lending Act of 1968.**

Don't get ripped off!

Acknowledgment

THIS IS MY first book, and I would like to thank God first. Next, I would like to thank all members of God's Final Warning Ministries and Pastor Alvin Fuller.

Then I would like to acknowledge my nephew, Brette Daniels, who always asks me year after year for his personal copy of *Buyers vs. Liars*. Latoya Chambers, Cynthia and Lacy Zachary, Kathy Wright, Fred and Judy Times, Joseph, Calvin and Alvin Jones, Russell Fagan and family, Mike Stillwell, Stephen Ferguson, Barbara, Ruby, Arthur Jr., Carl, Carolyn, and Norma Jean, Jewelene Rodgers, Dedra, Larry, Ricky and Shannon Lilly, Maya Mallegowda and David Codisoti, LaVonne Beverly and Ann Taylor, Carrie and Kevin Parker, Alin and Hinton Box, Stacy Harris, Andre Crosby, Gisele Crowther, Marco Scott, Fred, Tammi, Bridgette, Pete, Liza, Isaac, Javier, Brian and the entire staff at Academy Studios, Felicia Chestnut, Sandra O'Brien and Seat Belt Dan Wheeler at AGI, Calvin Alexis, Robert Nunn, Tim Blunt, James Martin "Jeep," Lonnie Wills, Kenneth Allan and Eduardo and Andrea, Charlotta and Jimmy Deamus, Wanda and Elisha Williams, Toshytome "Shy" Carter, Clarie Cohens, Shelia Riddlespringer, Mrs. Betty Williams, Pyton, Ferryne and Marcia Gatson, Frank and Kohl Byndloss, Linda and Alan Gold, Destiny, Shayla, Candace, Janice Hill and Amira Holmes, Janice and Janeile Cobbs, Jessica Adams, Maria Ferdico, Saroj Kalia, Rachel Rideau, Frank Anderson, Dolores Dyer, Kathryn Warner, Joyce, Rashida and Cynthia White, Heather Badial, Cynthia Holleman, Marilyn Jackson-Garrick, LaVerne Hillig-Hughes, Muriel Johnson, James Robbins, Frank Black, Sharon & C.J. Moret. Also to my entire family–Patricia, Hiawatha, Calvin, Phyllis, Ronnie, Veronica (my twin sister), Vernetta, Darrell, Flora, Supora, Aunt Cynthia, Broderick, Barry, Isshi Earhart, Marjorie and Shane Hefner, Beverly, Tina, Shemica, Tanji, Crystal, Jasmine, Erica Duncan, R.T., and Ukeshia, R.T. Jr., Curtis, Walter and Jonah Wilson, Antoinette, Mrs. Myra Jean Donnell, Elizabeth Watson, C.J. and Holly Torres and Pastor Stanley Alexander, Marcus and Tamika and other family members.

Special thanks to all of my teachers who inspired me daily, from H.S. Thompson Elementary, Pearl C. Anderson Junior High School and Wilmer-Hutchins High School, Mrs. Blair, Mrs. Booty, Mrs. Reed, Mrs. Dorothy, Mr. Kelly, Mr. Woods, Mrs. Green, Mrs. Lowery, Mrs. Pullum, Mr. Fisher, Coach Snyder, Coach Bruster, Coach Williams, Coach Givens, Ms. Fisher, Mrs. Bain, Coach Thomas, and Coach Tipps.

Special thanks to Erik Steen for the photo with your personal 10-speed bike, built by Erik Noren at Peacock Groove and Stephanie Hengst at Mt. Tamalpais, Calif. A special thanks to Brice Kahn and Ali from Cali for editing my book before publication.

Special thanks to Carolyn and Pattie Geiger with Pattie Speaks Biz or no Biz.

Thanks to Sherian "Sha" Smith for the photo of the author with the Lincoln High School Class of 1974, Dallas, Texas.

Thanks to Helen Ramos as my Vice President of Marketing/Partner Promoter.

Thanks to my cousin/investor with *Buyers vs. Liars,* Joyce White of Hayward, Calif. Thanks to my friend /investor Isaac Osuna.

A special thanks to Susie Drahn. When God made Susie, He created a very special person. She loves good-hearted people in life. Susie's heart is as big as they come.

To Susie, I thank you from the top and bottom of my heart for everything that you have done for me as a person. May God continue to bless you and may all of your wishes come true. You are a very special individual. Susie, we should call up Tina in Oregon and play another prank phone call on her. She's a lot of fun!

James "Jimmy" Zayas, thanks for your knowledge.

Richie, Christina Costello and especially Lori Blake, who told me, "Boy, you better get started on writing your book *Buyers vs Liars!*" Ha ha! Well, I finished!

Phyllis A. Alexander
Final Editor, Dallas, Texas

Thanks Xlibris
Yanni Fields, you gave me excellent customer service from the start.
David Lagahit, the cover design for my book is "tight." Thanks.
Ray Usman, thank you for connecting my Web site to Xlibris's Web Design.
Rachel Cruise, Your patience is very much appreciated. You are always happy when you say, "Sir, is there anything else that I can help you with?"

Introduction

FIRST OF ALL I would like to thank God for just keeping me here on earth as some of my family members has perished and is waiting on their judgment day. I'm Darmonica Alexander and the only thing in life I wanted to be was a professional football player in the National Football League (NFL). My dream was to catch the winning touch down in the Super Bowl with only a few seconds left on the game clock and to **be** selected into the Hall of Fame. Well that never happened.

Now I also heard that many athletes who did make the Pro's sold car and make over one hundred thousand dollars per year. I never made the NFL Professional Football team but I never lost my professionalism in life. There is something inside of me that makes me treat people exactly how I would want to be treated and is to tell me the truth and give me your best service. I carried this over with me into life and especially with the customers that I served in the automobile business. As you will see in this book there are customer who wrote me letters to back up my professional service that was rightly to them. Now I could make over one hundred thousands every year but I rather keep God's Ten commandments, which includes keeping the Sabbath day (Saturday) holy, than to chase that all mighty $$$ dollar!

See I really love God! Do you

THIS BOOK IS a consumer's information buying guide that the dealerships just don't want the public to see! I will give the consumers an inside look of what their monthly payments should look like before they ever arrive at the dealership. Pay attention on the negotiation and their monthly terms as the dealers will switch them on them in the final contract. This book is design for women based on everyday monthly payment. This consumer guide is for cars, trucks, motorcycles and any vehicles that get registration and licenses to operate. The automobile business wants the public to think that they are on their side when they are advertising on the television or radio, **well they are not**. Beware of their tricks.

My book is inspire by God to help the public as a whole because $aving money is what's it's all about! I will try to make this book very simple to read. If the consumer can read the monthly payment charts, and know how to negotiate the price it's easier.

When purchasing any vehicle there are several main things that make up your monthly payments. **First** of all is **the price** of the vehicle, **second** is the **term** (how many months that it takes to pay the vehicle off), **third** is the **percentage rate** (interest rates 7.9%), and **forth** the down payment (how much money to put down). The sales tax, doc fees and DMV fees must be paid, they are small but they pay a very important part of whole transaction.

To keep it simple for the consumers there are monthly payments charts throughout this information guide book. For an example of the rate: If a customer purchased a vehicle and they **sign the contract at 7.9% rates**, but the **bank approved the loan at 4.95% rate**, the dealership **suppose** to pass this rate to the customer and this will lower this monthly payments. Instead the dealership will keep these extra three points for their back end profit or they will give them to Finance Director for this commission. Now this is a clear violation of the **Truth in Lending Act**. So do yourself a favor and see if you can get an auto loan from your credit union or bank before you get to the dealership. This book is to make the consumers aware of the tricks that they have no idea of when purchasing a vehicle.

First make sure that the consumer NEGOIATE their price and sign the final NEGOIATED price before they go to the finance department and get a computer printout. Look at the method of the negotiation charts. Every time the dealer negotiates with the customer they will start out with very high offer and a high monthly payment. The consumer should do the reverse and offer low monthly payments. For an example: If the example chart in **Buyers vs. Liars** consumer's guide shows that the consumer's payments should will end up at **$400.00** per month for 60 months **and not 72 months**, start out with payments of $345.00. That is if the consumer knows their rates. If not still use this tactic, it works also. This is how they their mind games. So let's play

Remember this: Every time that they negotiate and give up $12.50 that = $750.00 added to your overall transaction/monthly payments. Every time that they negotiate and give up $25.00 that = $1500.00 added to your overall transaction/monthly payments. Every time that they negotiate and give up $50.00 that = $3,000.00 added to your overall transaction/monthly payments and etc.

Example: The list price is the MSRP price $20,102.22 and your rate is 7.9%, offer them $17,000.00 with monthly payments of $345.00. They will come back with the price $19,500.00 and month payments of $429.00 with. The consumer offers them $17,300.00 with payments of $365.00. They will offer $18,900.00 with monthly payments of $410.00. Tell them here is you final offer with $ 17,600.00

with payments of $ 385.00 and then tell them that if they can't do that then there is another vehicle that you were looking at and you will "be back." This will force the dealer to make a deal or not. Now watch for them to say O.K. you win at $385.00 monthly payments as they switch you monthly payments to 72 months. Make sure that this didn't happen! **This is one of their famous tricks that use at the end of the negotiation.**

Don't just give your money away to these dealerships, make them work for it. AGAIN DO NOT let them turn your **60 months payments** into **72 months payments. Its' a set up!**

This happens at the end of the consumer's final negotiation with the sales manager. Also watch out for the contract in the finance department to have 72 monthly payments on them as well. If this happens don't sign the contract until it correct. Remember that there are other dealerships to buy from and Buyers vs. Liars is here to assist the consumers on their monthly payments plan budget. Keep it simple!

Remember to study these charts and **FIGHT** FOR THE PRICE. FIGHT FOR THE **RATES** AND MOST OF ALL FIGHT FOR THE **MONTHLY PAYMENTS!**

The auto dealerships routinely takes the advantage of their so call valuable customers. For example, at one dealership where I worked, I discovered that the desk managers would automatically write the Hispanic and African American customers rates much higher than the White and Asian American customers. Hispanic and African American customers would get a 15% loan payment plan when they should have been written a 7.9% loan and the difference is huge $70 to $100 more on each monthly payment. The desk managers would also hide or smuggle a $2,495 extra in the service agreement without the customer knowing it.

Since I was the finance manager of that Department, I would change most of the customers' rates so their payments were about $70 lower than when they came in. The majority of my customer service agreement contracts were seven years and 100,000 miles with $0 deductible. When the White and Asian American deals came into the finance department, their rates were already lower from the beginning. This was clearly a disadvantage for the minority customers.

When dealerships are hiding the consumer's unauthorized monthly payment, without disclosed the true facts to the consumers it's a serious crime, this is a clear violation of the Truth in Lending Act. That's why I'm serving public notice: Your hard-earned money is being ripped off by car dealers. As new technology brings about the next wave of hybrid and electric vehicles, you owe it to yourself to read *Buyers vs. Liars: Secrets of the Auto Dealerships,* so you can beat the dealerships at their own game. All of their tricks will be exposed when the you know what to look for and demand **A COMPUTER PRINTOUT!**

Truth in Lending Act

The Truth in Lending Act (TILA) of 1968 is a federal law designed to protect consumers in credit transactions. It requires a disclosure of key terms of the lending arrangements and all costs. The goal is to make it easier for the consumer to compare the lending terms among several financial institutions. Lenders must disclose the annual percentage rate (APR), or cost of credit to the consumer. Lenders also must disclose other costs such as origination fees and discount points.

October 12, 2008

Mr. Darmonica Alexander
El Sobrante, CA 94803

Dear Darmonica,

This letter is to thank you for helping me with the incredibly challenging process of buying a new car with out "getting ripped off".

When I saw your book "Buyers vs. Liars" Secrets of the Auto Dealerships" I knew that I had found a great guide in buying a new car right.

You walked me through the pages that showed me how much car I could afford and how to get to the bottom line of dealer costs and find just the right deal. You even went with me to the dealer and showed me step by step what the book illustrated as examples of what to ask for and negotiate.

Thanks to the lessons from your book I ended up with a deal on a new car that I never would have dreamed of getting prior. Your help and knowledge was very much appreciated.

I strongly recommend this book for anyone who is about to buy a car. Knowledge is power and this book is "Powerful!!"

Thank you again,

Alan and Linda Gold

America: Making History in the White House

God Bless America

**We are all proud to be Americans
of the United States of America.**

The American Auto Dealerships' Bailout

Who Will Pay Back the First $13.4 Billion Auto Loan?
Another Auto Loan of $4 Billion Later!

The public once again will be burdened by the cost. But this time, the public is prepared–with a perfect buying guide to keep them from getting ripped off by any dealership, new or used, auto, motorcycle, boat, jet ski, etc. More than 10 million vehicles are sold every year, and this year the economy is off its target. This economy is tightening its grip on every dollar that is spent out of a family's budget. Where is your bailout?

The bailout from TARP (Troubled Asset Relief Program) will assist the American auto dealerships, but citizens can take control and save themselves *thousand of dollars* before any dealership rips them off!

This book, *Buyers vs. Liars,* is a very important business guide for the public to use effectively. Don't enter the dealership without knowing this information.

The American consumers really need to learn the math concept in this book to increase their purchasing power.

It's very important to learn the math structure for purchasing used or new vehicles. This is a must! Stand up and become a smart purchaser and consumer. Remember, this math concept is for all vehicles new/used and the future as well. What a clever buying guide!

Now, Pay Attention or Pay Extra.

Chapter 1

Valuable Customers

THE MAJORITY OF the American automobile industries will never be honest with their "valuable customers" because they would lose money. Many dealerships across America earned billions of dollars through profits from millions of customers. Come to think of it, the statement above should read like this: "Many dealerships across America have stolen and ripped off millions of their customers by secretly hiding the customers' hard-earned money." This is a violation of the customers' rights, and they are not aware of this crime committed against them. The extra money that the customer is losing at the dealership makes it hard to save money for the future. Many Americans were straining to put gas in their vehicle due to the suffering economy. The price of eggs, butter, bread and public transportation has gone up as well. The gas price has gone down for the moment and will America be prepared when it return? This book is to make that the future generation of consumer will be more educated when it come to purchasing vehicles and $aving money at the same time.

The reason that this self-help information guide needs to be published is because customers are routinely lied to and ripped off because they don't know what they are up against with the dealerships. *The dealers play dirty little tricks to confuse the customer by mixing up numbers with various monthly terms. That's why* Buyers vs. Liars *is about numbers itself.*

I want to make sure American automobile buyers know how to secure the best deal for the next wave of hybrids, electric and conventional vehicles.

First, when purchasing a vehicle, try to pick the best vehicle with the best resale value for the family (Honda is my choice), whether it's an SUV, a Jeep Wrangler, or a VW Bug. Try to have two in mind, and keep an eye out for the best vehicle for your money. Remember this: *nice things aren't cheap, and cheap things aren't nice. Pay a little more and get a better vehicle you will love it in the end.* Go to the dealerships when they are closed and look around. Compare the different types of vehicles with the same equipment, for example, the Honda Accord EX and VW Rabbit. Get the MSRP price off the vehicle, go home, and compare the values and resale value on the Internet. Get a preapproved loan from your credit union or bank. Remember, *the down payment is normally the dealership's profit.* Keep the down payment out of the transaction at first. Do all your financing with your credit union or bank, unless the dealership has a lower interest rate. Remember to always fight for the price.

Follow the *six secrets of the auto dealership* step-by-step because buying a vehicle can be very tricky if you don't know how much customers are being ripped off. Remember, if you have good or bad credit, you must always *fight for the price.*

Here are six secrets that the consumer should be looking out for when purchasing a new/used vehicle. By following the secrets the consumer will have a better chance of saving extra money by knowing what to look for in their transaction.

1. The price — $ Amount you negotiate on
2. The rates — APR (annual percentage rate 5.95%)
3. The terms — $59 + 1 = 60$ months (how many months to pay it off)
4. The service agreement — Warranty (Hidden items)
5. The payment — $500.00 (if you don't know, rip off time)
6. The lease contact — If you have money to waste, this is for you. If this is the best you can do go for it.

Doc fee: Documentations fee

DMV (Department of Motor Vehicle): State fees for registration of the vehicle (fees differ from state to state)

Sales tax: Government tax on a sold vehicle (8.25%)

Total price: Total price if customer pays cash

Amount financed: Amount charged that the customer pays to the finance company according to their interest rates.

Finance charges: Amount charged and amount borrowed on the loan until the vehicle is paid off.

Remember that the dealerships are the Pro's at these games, but Buyers vs. Liars will assist the public with a little more information to narrow the gap against these unethical dealerships. Once the consumers have learned the dealer's concepts on purchasing a vehicle, in the future it this buying guide will become the consumer's best friend!

FIGHT FOR THE PRICE

Now Buyers vs. Liars is not here to bash the auto dealership, it is to help the public get an honest and a fair deal without getting ripped off. This book and consumer's guide is a future reference many generations to follow. Now millions of consumers can know the truth about their hard earned money with it comes to their vehicle monthly payments and transaction.

Invoice

VIN # *****GJ***J****** 2008 Honda Accord SE

Unit price   **$17,860.96**

2010

Total unit price   **$17,860.96**

Manufacturer's Suggested Retail Price (MSRP)   **$20,102.22**

This is an example of using a made-up invoice instead of a real dealership's invoice for legal reasons. The strategy is to show the buyer how to "Fight for the Price".

In this charts below, purchase price is located next to the price ($17,860.96), the monthly payment is located under Amount $400.00, or terms is located under Due / Start 59+1 =60 months (how many years it takes to pay off the loan off).

		***** Payment Schedule *****	
Price	17,860.96		
Accessories	.00		
Doc Fee	35.00	**Due / Starting**	**Amount**
Sales Tax	1,476.42		
Service Agreement	.00	59 **12-30-09**	$400.00
Cash Price	19,372.38	1 **11-30-14**	$400.00
DMV Fees	389.00	**Amount Financed**	**19,761.38**
Insurance Premiums	.00	**APR**	**7.93**
Total Purchase	19,761.38	**Finance Charge**	**4,238.62**
		Total of Payments	**24,000.00**
Trade-In	.00	Total Sales Price	24,000.00
Less Pay-Off	.00		
Net Trade-In	.00		
Deferred Down	.00		
Amount Paid Now	.00		
Total Down payment	.00		

The total price is located next to total of payments $24,000.00 (with down payment) and total sales price is located next to total sales price $24,000.00 (if no down payment).

		***** Payment Schedule *****	
Price	20,102.22		
Accessories	.00		
Doc Fee	35.00	**Due / Starting**	**Amount**
Sales Tax	1,661.32		
Service Agreement	.00	59 **12-30-09**	$450.00
Cash Price	21,798.34	1 **11-30-14**	$450.00
DMV Fees	433.00	**Amount Financed**	**22,231.54**
Insurance Premiums	.00	**APR**	**7.93**
Total Purchase	22,231.54	**Finance Charge**	**4,768.46**
		Total of Payments	**27,000.00**
Trade-In	.00	Total Sales Price	27,000.00
Less Pay-Off	.00		
Net Trade-In	.00		
Deferred Down	.00		
Amount Paid Now	.00		
Total Down Payment	.00		

Both charts are the same except the purchase price is different. One price is the Invoice price $17,860.96 and the other one is the MSRP price $20,102.22. The difference in the monthly payments is $50.00 and the total of payments, is $3,000.00. This is why Buyers vs. Liars is encouraging the consumers to fight for the price and use this buying guide.

"Fight for the Price."

Once the dealership has captured your attention with those low monthly payments, you get all excited and pack the family and head for the dealership, be very careful and don't let them get you for all of your hard earned money. Once the buyers have met their salesperson and explained that they came regarding the television ad, they later find out that they are no longer looking at the advertised vehicle. If you are looking for the ad vehicle, usually the salesperson will steer the buyer from the advertised vehicle because the he or she will not make a huge profit–only about $100. Now it's a different story. They want to see how much money you have to put down and how much you can spend per month. Do not tell them about a down payment, because the down payment is usually their profit.

Then look at the MSRP (*manufacturer's suggested retail price*). The MSRP is not what you want to pay; the *invoice* price is what you want to pay or $200 to $500 over that *invoice* price for the dealership's profit. But the poor quality manufacturer automobile or the crappy vehicles pay $100.00 or less over cost and remember that 10 years and 100,000 warranty that comes with vehicle! You are going to need! I know the economy is tough but pay a little more and get a better vehicle. If this is your best for your budget, go for it!

The Addendum Sticker

The manufacturer's suggested retail price (MSRP) is located on the side of the window. In some states, there are *addendum stickers that are added to the price on the MSRP* (the asking price). Sometimes, the markup is $2,500 or more.

Example: The Invoice price is $41,500.00, the MSRP price is $45,000.00 + addendum price is $2500.00 = the selling price $47,500.00

Now the dealers are sell this vehicle for a $6,000.00 profit from the customer.

I was told that addendum stickers were added to the vehicle in order to help out the buyers who are trading in their vehicle, and they need room to help them get out of their trade vehicle. That is not totally true. The addendum markup is just another way for the dealership to have more room on the price of their vehicles.

Example: The invoice price is $41,500.00 and the list selling price is $47,500.00 How much profit are you willing to give a dealership for your new vehicle?

The customer purchases a warranty or extended service agreement or maybe a DVD system this will increase the dealer's backend profit of $2,000.00. Now the dealer's total transaction profit is $8,000.00 just from one customer. How much are you willing to give up

Go Green

and

Stay Clean

When the dealers see you emotion about how you "just love that car" that all they need to know. Don't let them see your emotion, let them see education about your finances. This would be an American dream, but most of the dealerships don't really care about your finances.

Negotiating on Television Ads

When the automobile dealerships are advertising their product, you can bet that the low price on the television is not the price of the vehicle in the video. Example: If any dealership such as Ford, Honda, Chevrolet, or Mercedes-Benz advertises new vehicles for only $199 a month for 24 or 36 months, normally it's a leased vehicle. They might not say it, but it's usually the case. Most of the time, the dealership will show customers a top-of-the-line vehicle on television, with the sports kit, leather seats, nice rims, and all the other extras. If you could just freeze the television frame and read the fine print, you would find out that the vehicle price was on a basic vehicle and not the vehicle that was shown in the television advertisement. The fine print reads something like, "The vehicle shown was the EX model for $35,000 and tax, title, and license not included."

Let's look at $199 or $200 monthly payments and see just how much vehicle a buyer can purchase with $0 down. You can get a *hoopty* or put about $8,000 down in order to get these payments. You can lease and pay half for the usage of a lease vehicle and be back at the dealer in three years and do this over and over again!

Example: Just look at the chart provided for you with $200.00 monthly payments.

Monthly payments	Number of months	Purchase price	Percentage rate
$200.00	24 mos.	$4,161.58	2.9%
$200.00	36 mos.	$6,068.47	3.9%
$200.00	48 mos.	$7,823.43	4.9 %
$200.00	60 mos.	$8,899.58	7.9 %

Now can you see a better and brighter picture of the vehicle price? If you were purchasing a new vehicle, you would know that something is wrong with this picture of $200 payments. That is why this book is called *Buyers vs. Liars.*

When a dealership advertises **$199** and **$0** down payment and a low percentage rate for 24 or 36 months, the payment schedule chart below will show you how much of a vehicle you can expect to spend on a purchase price that includes all fees. This is a lease or a purchase. Example:

A vehicle priced at **$4,161.58** at 24 months = **$200.00** monthly payments at **2.95%**

A vehicle priced at **$6,082.47** at 36 months = **$200.00** monthly payments   at **3.99%**

Taxes are based on California state taxes at 8.25%.

Price	4,161.58	***** Payment Schedule *****	
Accessories	.00		
Doc fee	35.00	Due / Starting	Amount
Sales tax	346.21		
Service agreement	.00	23 12-30-09	$200.00
Cash price	4,542.79	1 11-30-11	$200.00
DMV fees	113.00	Amount financed	4,655.79
Insurance premiums	.00	APR	2.95
Total purchase	4,655.79	Finance charge	144.21
		Total of payments	4,800.00
		Total sales price	4,800.00

****

Price	6,082.47	***** Payment Schedule *****	
Accessories	.00		
Doc fee	35.00	Due / Starting	Amount
Sales tax	504.69		
Service agreement	.00	35 12-30-09	$200.00
Cash price	6,622.16	1 11-3012	$200.00
DMV fees	153.00	Amount financed	6,775.16
Insurance premiums	.00	APR	3.99
Total purchase	6,775.16	Finance charge	424.84
		Total of payments	7,200.00
		Total sales price	7,200.00

With this information in the payment schedule chart, you can see how the dealerships attract many customers to fall for the lower advertised monthly payments that have a catch to it–just to rip customers off.

TV Advertising: Read the Fine Print

The dealer's advertising shows the low payments to lure the public to their dealership with deceiving lies in the small print. Listed on the TV advertising price was **$17,495**. Now the sales price is **$11,995**, and this price is below wholesale price. The payments are only **$169** a month, *so call us right now* at 1-555-XXX-8888. The trick is in the small print below.

Vin number 2564 There is only one vehicle at this price, and this is for 60 months of payments and with 5.95% approval. The customer must pay for doc fees and DMV fees, sales tax and any finance charges with $5,000 down.

****

This is what the public doesn't know, and here is what the dealerships are saying and what they really mean. The key is that the customer must qualify for the 5.95% first in order to get the monthly payments. Here is the deception: the doc fees, $55.00; DMV fees, $165.00; sales tax, $1,397.14; and finance charges, $2,502.84 with $5,000.00 down payment. Once the customer adds up all of these charges and fees, the payment is around $226.66 monthly. This is about $4,119.98 out of the customer's pocket; this is where the salesperson will switch (bait and switch) the customers to a different vehicle and sale the customer a vehicle of the salesman's choice. This is just to get the customers from the TV set to their dealership. This book and information guide of *Buyers vs. Liars* is here to assist the public in identifying savings that are overlooked.

Payment Schedule Charts at 5.9%
for 60 Months

This is what the dealers want you to see and believe about their advertising. This is a naked chart, with 5.9% and $160.56 for 60 months ($5,000.00 down).

		***** Payment Schedule *****	
Price	9,633.65		
Accessories	.00		
Doc fee	.00	Due / Starting	Amount
Dealer smog	.00		
Sales tax	.00		
Service agreement	.00	59 12-30-09	160.56
Cash price	9,633.65	1 11-30-14	160.56
DMV fees	.00	Amount financed	9,633.65
Insurance premiums	.00	APR	5.9
Total purchase	.00	Finance charges	
		Total of payments	
		Total sales price	

****

		***** Payment Schedule *****	
Price	16,880.02		
Accessories	.00		
Doc fee	55.00	Due / Starting	Amount
Dealer smog	.00		
Sales tax	1,397.14		
Service agreement	.00	59 12-30-09	266.66
Cash price	18,332.16	1 11-30-14	266.66
DMV fees	165.00	Amount financed	13,497.16
Insurance premiums	.00	APR	5.9
Total purchase	18,497.16	Finance charges	2,502.84
		Total of payments	16,000.00
		Total sales price	21,000.00
Trade-in	.00		
Less payoff	.00		
Net trade-in	.00		
Deferred down	.00		
Amount paid now	5,000.00		
Total down payment	5,000.00		

In reality, the above payments schedule chart is what the customer doesn't see. He/she must qualify for the 5.9% rate before any transaction begins. Take a look at the extra fees that are in small print. Look at the doc fees, sales tax, DMV fees, finance charges, and the down payment that totaled to $6,366.35. Don't be fooled!

Example: Advertised as $19,966

Purchasing a vehicle from the dealership's newspaper advertisement can be negotiated as well. There is some profit in some of the advertised vehicles. The buyer can offer the dealership $19,654.96, and if the dealership goes for it, the dealership wants to move vehicles. If the dealer doesn't agree, still take the deal.

Price	19,654.96
Accessories	.00
Doc fee	35.00
Sales tax	1,624.42
Service agreement	.00
Cash price	21,314.38
DMV fees	425.00
Insurance premiums	.00
Total purchase	21,739.38
Trade-in	.00
Less payoff	.00
Net trade-in	.00
Deferred down	.00
Amount paid now	
Total down payment	

* Payment Schedule * 4.9%

Due / Starting		Amount
47	12-30-09	500.00
1	11-30-13	500.00

Amount financed	21,739.38
APR	4.94
Finance charges	2,260.62
Total of payments	24,000.00
Total sales price	24,000.00

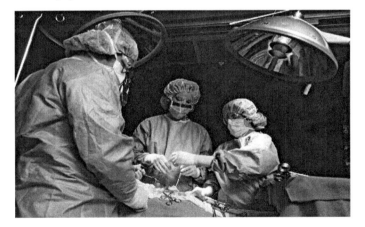

What happened here? This customer let the salesperson tell him that the newspaper ads' vehicle has already been sold, and they paid too much for their new vehicle. I demanded to see the ID to see if it matched the same ID number that was in the newspaper. Girl, they lied! If you don't read the *Buyers vs. Liars'* information guidebook, you could be lying here as well.

Manufacturer Rebate to the Public or Cash Back

Manufacturer rebate is a rebate from the automobile manufacturer that is given to the public, but the money is given to the customer in a form of a down payment in the buyer's contract. This rebate will be added to the purchase price of the vehicle to be taxed, and then it will be used for the customer's down payment. This is how it works. Dealers hide the extra "service agreement" in customers' payments.

Example: A rebate of $2,000, and the vehicle purchase price was $15,000 with $0 down payment. The purchase price of $15,000 + $2,000 = $17,000. Total purchase must be taxed, and then the $2,000 rebate will be a down payment.

Notice that there is an extra item. A "service agreement" of $1,595 was smuggled into the customer's monthly payment without the customer's authorization.

Price	17,000.00
Accessories	.00
Doc fee	35.00
Dealer smog	29.00
Sales tax	1,407.78
Service agreement	1,595.00
Cash price	20,066.78

* Payment Schedule * 12.54%		
Due / Starting		Amount
59	12-30-09	$406.97
1	11-30-14	$406.97

DMV fees	333.00
Insurance premiums	.00
Total purchase	20,399.78

Amount financed	18,339.78
APR	12.54
Finance charge	6,078.42
Total of payments	24,418.20
Total sales price	26,418.20

Trade-in	.00
Less payoff	.00
Net trade-in	.00
Deferred down	.00
Amount paid now	2,000.00
Total down payment	2,000.00

Combining the invoice price, interest rates and the monthly terms makes up the buyer's monthly payment. The down payment should be added after the buyer has determined the price. Remember to fight for the price before the rebate is added to that price. If you have the down payment, take the low rates. In some cases, don't take the rebate. Tell the dealer you want seven years and 100,000 miles and $0 deductible service agreement for $800 instead of the $1,595 service agreement.

The manufacturer's rebates or cash back add to your monthly payments

Example: Monthly payments 350.00 + payments below

1,000 = 16.00 + Tax	6,000 = 100.00 + Tax
2,000 = 33.00 + Tax	7,000 = 116.00 + Tax
3,000 = 50.00 + Tax	8,000 = 133.00 + Tax
4,000 = 66.00 + Tax	9,000 = 150.00 + Tax
5,000 = 83.00 + Tax	10,000 = 160.00 + Tax

This chart is based on 60 months payment plan.

Rebates/Cash Back vs. Down Payment

The rebate gives the customers a down payment that helps them out as far as banks are concerned. In most cases, some customers need the rebate to show the bank more money as a down payment. This payment chart shows $2,000 down.

****

Price	15,000.00	***Payment Schedule ***	**12.51%**
Accessories	.00		
Doc fee	35.00	**Due / Starting**	**Amount**
Dealer smog	29.00		
Sales tax	1,242.78		
Service agreement	1,595.00	59 12-30-09	357.97
Cash price	17,901.78	1 11-30-14	357.97
DMV fees	6.00	Amount financed	15,907.78
Insurance premiums	.00	APR	12.51
Total purchase	17,907.78	Finance charge	5,570.42
		Total of payments	21,478.20
Trade-in	.00	Total sales price	23,478.20
Less payoff	.00		
Net trade-in	.00		
Deferred down	.00		
Amount paid now	2,000.00		
Total down payment	2,000.00		

Do not tell the salesperson how much money you have to put down. Just remember to keep your eyes open. Look at the next two payment schedule charts and look at the difference between the payments with a $2,000 rebate and the customer's own down payment. There is approximately $50 difference per month that adds up to nearly $3,000 difference. *Fight for the price.*

With Down Payment vs. Rebate or Cash Back

This payment chart shows the customer's $2,000.00 down with a payment of $185.97.

Price	10,000.00	***** Payment Schedule *****	
Accessories	.00		
Doc fee	35.00	Due / Starting	Amount
Dealer smog	29.00		
Sales tax	803.28		
Service agreement	.00	59 12-30-09	185.97
Cash price	10,867.28	1 11-30-14	185.97
DMV fees	6.00	Amount financed	8,873.28
Insurance premiums	.00	APR	9.28
Total purchase	10,873.28	Finance charge	2,284.92
		Total of payments	11,158.20
Trade-in	.00	Total sales price	13,158.20
Less payoff	.00		
Net trade-in	.00		
Deferred down	.00		
Amount paid now	2,000.00		
Total down payment	2,000.00		

****

Price	12,000.00	***** Payment Schedule *****	
Accessories	.00		
Doc fee	35.00	Due / Starting	Amount
Dealer smog	29.00		
Sales tax	995.28		
Service agreement	.00	59 12-30-09	230.97
Cash price	13,059.28	1 11-30-14	230.97
DMV fees	6.00	Amount financed	11,065.28
Insurance premiums	.00	APR	9.28
Total purchase	13,065.28	Finance charge	2,792.92
		Total of payments	13,858.20
Trade-in	.00	Total sales price	15,858.20
Less payoff	.00		
Net trade-in	.00		
Deferred down	.00		
Amount paid now	2,000.00		
Total down payment	2,000.00		

By paying your own down payment, you will save on your monthly payment. The bottom chart shows a $2,000.00 rebate that is added on the $10,000.00 to be taxed. Remember, payments are about $50.00 higher than the top chart. Take the lower rate of 2.95%.

If the dealer offers a lower percentage rate, make sure that your payments are lower.

The Price

When you go to the dealership to purchase a vehicle, the salesperson will write the deal on a standard form known as a four-square sheet. This four-square is for your information, such as name and address information. Then the four square is as follows: (1) price of the vehicle, (2) down payment, (3) monthly payments, and (4) a vehicle to be traded.

If you have read the *Buyers vs. Liars'* information guide, you should tell the dealer that you have no vehicle to trade, and you qualify for 2.95% rate with payments of $450.00 for 60 months and no money down. Watch out for the desk manager trying to play as if you are uneducated when it comes to numbers. Next, the dealer will come back with something stupid to try to throw you off with numbers, such as $750.00 monthly payments with 48 months and $3,000.00 down. The vehicle's MSRP cost will be $29,515.18. Don't let them know that you have $5,000.00 for a down payment. Notice the price that customer is offering is $22,868.24 (+ $5,000.00 down). The total offer is $27,868.24, including the down payment. This includes $200.00 over invoice cost. Understand this concept! This is just to let the dealer know that you are not playing his price game, and that you have the control of this deal from the beginning. You should mark all over the four-square and mark the original request. Ask to see the invoice cost.

This guidebook will keep you informed from the beginning of this transaction. The dealer is not in control; he/she is now just trying to make a deal.

		***** Payment Schedule *****		
Price	22,868.24			
Accessories	.00			
Doc fee	55.00	Due / Starting		Amount
Dealer smog	29.00			
Sales tax	1,893.55			
Service agreement	.00	59	12-30-09	450.00
Cash price	24,845.79	1	11-30-14	450.00
DMV fees	204.00	Amount financed		25,049.79
Insurance premiums	.00	APR		2.95
Total purchase	25,049.79	Finance charges		1,950.21
		Total of payments		27,000.00
		Total sales price		27,000.00
Trade-in	.00			
Less payoff	.00			
Net trade-in	.00			
Deferred down	.00			
Amount paid now	.00			
Total down payment	.00			

Here Are the Dealer's Tricks!

The dealer will send the manager or closer back out with the original four-square or on the back of the original four-square with numbers like the ones below.

The dealer will change the terms and make them shorter terms, such as 48 months and with a different rate of 4.9%, with payments of $750.00. The dealer wants the customer to "see higher monthly payments." The dealer payments are $200.00 higher per month. Take control of the situation by marking all over their four-square and looking at all parts of the four-square.

The customer must take more control by marking out the terms and changing it back to 60 months. Then ask to see the invoice and the offer of 2% over cost or $200-$500; this depends on the vehicle (e.g., Mercedes-Benz).

Price	29,515.18
Accessories	.00
Doc fee	35.00
Sales tax	2,437.89
Service agreement	.00
Cash price	31,988.07

***** Payment Schedule *****

Due / Starting		Amount
47	12-30-09	750.00
1	11-30-13	750.00

DMV fees	621.00
Insurance premiums	.00
Total purchase	32,609.07

Amount financed	29,609.07
APR	4.94
Finance charges	3,390.93
Total of payments	33,000.00
Total sales price	36,000.00

Trade-in	.00
Less payoff	.00
Net trade-in	.00
Deferred down	.00
Amount paid now	3,000.00
Total down payment	3,000.00

After getting the invoice and agreeing on 2% over cost, look at the payments and then tell them that you want a seven years and 100,000 miles warranty with $0 deductible. Remember to ask to see the cost of the service agreement. The customer should pay around $800.00 for this contract. Stick to the original payment, then add the down payment into the agreed price; now calculate your monthly payments. After they come back with (example) $556.00, tell the dealer that they have a deal with monthly payments of $550.00. Squeeze the dealer for every penny.

Chapter 2

Credit Report

EXCELLENT CREDIT. WHEN purchasing a new or used vehicle from a dealership, the majority of the buyers will need some financial assistance from an institution such as a credit union or bank. There are three credit reporting agencies that are used to determine the buyer's credit buying power – TransUnion, Experian, and Equifax. These reports will determine if the buyer will get the lowest interest rate available on the market, such as rates as low as 0%, 2.9%, 3.9%, or 4.9%.

Good credit. Having good credit will open every door in the world of spending. Good credit is nothing but power. The economy has changed many lives. Protect your credit, and it will protect you. Some buyers are qualified for **5.9%**, **7.9%**, **9%**, **11.9%**, and **13.9%**. There are some circumstances where many buyers have bad credit due to bankruptcy, slow paying habits, or the economy's rising cost of crude oil and the housing market.

Bad Credit. Slow (late) payments, large amounts of unpaid bills due to child care costs, the job market, or even a divorce. This may cause a person's excellent credit to be turned upside down. Bad credit can be repaired by paying off some of those charged-off accounts. Receive your credit reports by contacting Experian, TransUnion, and Equifax. With these hard times, one can start repairing their credit with **15.9%**, **17.9%**, and **19.9%**.

Identity theft. There are people who prey upon others by stealing their credit information and using it to purchase goods. They will dig through your trash cans, retrieve information from the Internet, and even from gas station credit machines by using a certain strip that gets your information from the credit booth. Protect your credit by putting as little information as possible on the Internet. Protect your credit . . .

The court will give your client three to four years of prison time for this crime. Tell your client that there are hundred of scam artist lurking around the world. His punishment is no scam. The Ten Commandments states that thou shalt not steal.

Preapproved Loan

Preapproved loans can be obtained from your credit union, bank, or any lending institution. Search for the lowest rate. When going to the dealership, take this guideline information book with you and let them know that you have a preapproved loan. When a qualified buying customer asks the dealer to see the computer printout, and if the dealer refuses, the customer should just stand up and walk out. The desk manager will panic, and then they will do almost anything to keep from losing that deal, especially when you have a *preapproved* loan. *The price becomes the main focus of the negotiation when the customer has his or her own loan.*

Women Buying Power

Approved

$45,000.00 2008 Honda Accord EX

(Tax and license included)

First-Time Buyer Program

The first-time buyer program is designed for customers who are purchasing a vehicle for the very first time, are using credit for the purchase and looking to build their credit for the future.

In 2009, it has been very hard for bankers to give consumer loans to purchase new or used vehicles. The best thing to do is to try to get a preapproved loan from a family member's credit union. In today's world, sometimes it is best to go to the auction and purchase a good, reliable vehicle with low miles, such as a Honda or Toyota. If you have good credit with $3,000 to $5,000 of credit history on your credit report, ask the dealer to send your loan for a preapproval from the bank first to see what rate they will approve you for. Now the dealer is going to try to make you drive the vehicle home; that's their job. Once the approval comes back, make sure that you see the approval rates. Do not be afraid to go to another dealer to get a lower rate. The rates you want are around 7% or 9%. Fight for the rates. If approved, keep your payments very low. This is not the time to be greedy. Most of all, don't do it alone. Take a male friend or your father with you. The dealer has not learned to be honest with their customers. Keep payments around $250 per month.

Dancing with joy! This is the real American Dream—I'm so happy.

A Co-signer

A co-signer is a family member who will sign with their great credit to help another family member on purchasing a vehicle. The co-signer is the responsible member for the purchased vehicle. Now the dealer will use this to write the contract at a higher rate because of the other member's bad credit. This is where the credit union will come in handy. Try to sign up the family member with the credit union; if not, see if the credit union will take the deal with you and the family member together. Make sure that there is GAP insurance that is included with your loan; this is a must. The new hybrid and electric vehicles are on the market, and the automakers are going to try to get as much money from the customer as they can. This book, *Buyers vs. Liars*, will start a new revolution on how Americans will purchase vehicles without getting ripped off.

Watch out for the straw purchase!

This is where the dealer gets the co-signer to sign for the vehicle without the family member on the contract. This does nothing for the family member's credit. *Don't do it.* Go to an auction with about $2,000 and purchase a used Honda or Toyota vehicle; they are great vehicles.

This is good news to co-sign for our sister-in-law!

All across America, families pray for a better economy. This book, *Buyers vs. Liars*, has a solution for any citizen who wants to purchase a vehicle. This book saves the customers extra money that they might not have seen because they just don't know where the dealers were hiding their hard-earned money.

Excellent Credit vs. Not-so-good Credit

Price	19,654.96		* Payment Schedule *	4.95%
Accessories	.00			
Doc fee	35.00		Due / Starting	Amount
Sales tax	1,624.42			
Service agreement	.00	47	12-30-09	500.00
Cash price	21,314.38	1	11-30-13	500.00
DMV fees	425.00		Amount financed	21,739.38
Insurance premiums	.00		APR	4.9
Total purchase	21,739.38		Finance charges	2,260.62
			Total of payments	24,000.00
Trade-in	.00		Total sales price	24,000.00
Less payoff	.00			
Net trade-in	.00			
Deferred down	.00			
Amount paid now	.00			
Total down payment	.00			

****

Price	19,654.96		* Payment Schedule *	13.00%
Accessories	.00			
Doc fee	35.00		Due / Starting	Amount
Sales tax	1,624.42			
Service agreement	.00	59	12-30-09	500.00
Cash price	21,314.38	1	11-30-14	500.00
DMV fees	425.00		Amount financed	21,739.38
Insurance premiums	.00		APR	13.00
Total purchase	21,739.38		Finance charges	8,260.62
			Total of payments	30,000.00
			Total sales price	30,000.00
Trade-in	.00			
Less payoff	.00			
Net trade-in	.00			
Deferred down	.00			
Amount paid now	.00			
Total down payment	.00			

Look at the customer with excellent credit versus a customer with good credit. The difference is $6,000, but the customer with excellent credit pays one year less of payments.

Price	27,415.31
Accessories	.00
Doc fee	55.00
Dealer smog	29.00
Sale tax	2,268.69
Service agreement	.00
Cash price	29,768.00

DMV fees	232.00
Insurance premiums	.00
Total purchase	30,000.00

Trade-in	.00
Less payoff	.00
Net trade-in	.00
Deferred down	.00
Amount paid now	.00
Total down payment	.00

***** Payment Schedule *****

Due / Starting		Amount
59	12-30-09	500.00
1	11-30-14	500.00

Amount financed	30,000.00
APR	0.00
Finance charges	.00
Total of payments	30,000.00
Total sales price	30,000.00

****

Price	17,121.16
Accessories	.00
Doc fee	35.00
Dealer smog	.00
Sales tax	1,415.38
Service agreement	.00
Cash price	18,571.54

DMV fees	166.00
Insurance premiums	.00
Total purchase	18,737.54

Trade-in	.00
Less payoff	.00
Net trade-in	.00
Deferred down	.00
Amount paid now	.00
Total down payment	.00

***** Payment Schedule *****

Due / Starting		Amount
59	12-30-09	500.00
1	11-30-14	500.00

Amount financed	18,737.54
APR	19.95
Finance charges	11,262.46
Total of payments	30,000.00
Total sales price	30,000.00

The charts show excellent credit versus poor credit, and it is about $10,000 more for the vehicle that is purchased by the customer with excellent credit. The customer with poor credit pays more finance charges.

Price	39,765.17
Accessories	.00
Doc fee	55.00
Dealer smog	29.00
Sales tax	3,287.55
Service agreement	.00
Cash price	43,136.12
DMV fees	313.00
Insurance premiums	.00
Total purchase	43,449.72
Trade-in	.00
Less payoff	.00
Net trade-in	.00
Deferred down	.00
Amount paid now	.00
Total down payment	.00

***** Payment Schedule *****

Due / Starting		Amount
59	12-30-09	800.00
1	11-30-14	800.00

Amount financed	43,449.72
APR	3.9
Finance charges	4,550.28
Total of payments	48,000.00
Total sales price	48,000.00

****

Price	31,955.98
Accessories	.00
Doc fee	35.00
Dealer smog	29.00
Sales tax	2,641.64
Service agreement	.00
Cash price	34,661.62
DMV fees	262.00
Insurance premiums	.00
Total purchase	34,923.62
Trade-in	.00
Less payoff	.00
Net trade-in	.00
Deferred down	.00
Amount paid now	.00
Total down payment	.00

***** Payment Schedule *****

Due / Starting		Amount
59	12-30-09	800.00
1	11-30-14	800.00

Amount financed	34,923.62
APR	13.9
Finance charges	13,676.38
Total of payments	48,000.00
Total sales price	48,000.00

The charts above show the difference between the two 60-month terms and that the customer with excellent credit can purchase $7,809.19 more vehicle. The bottom chart pays $8,574.43 more in interest at a rate of 13%, with a lower vehicle purchase price.

Chapter 3

Getting Ripped Off: Hidden Secretly

SERVICE AGREEMENT. THIS is where the dealership hides your money! Look for extra items to make sure that an extra service agreement is not smuggled into your monthly payments. Look at the service agreement line. In the example below, the extra amount is $2,495 added to the customer's monthly payments, without authorization. This is a violation.

Price	15,000.00
Accessories	.00
Doc fee	35.00
Sales tax	1,240.39
Service agreement	2,495.00
Cash price	18,770.39
DMV fees	333.00
Insurance premiums	.00
Total purchase	19,103.39
Trade-in	.00
Less payoff	.00
Net trade-in	.00
Deferred down	.00
Amount paid now	5,000.00
Total down payment	5,000.00

***** Payment Schedule *****

Due / Starting		Amount
59	12-30-09	292.76
1	11-30-14	292.76

Amount financed	14,103.39
APR	9.00
Finance charge	3,462.21
Total of payments	17,565.60
Total sales price	22,565.60

The sales manager is violating the Truth-in-Lending Acts. Stealing the customers' money right from under their noses is still a crime. Read the book *Buyers vs. Liars* and watch out for their tricks. These crimes need to be reported.

Price	30,000.00
Accessories	.00
Doc fee	35.00
Dealer smog	29.00
Sales tax	2,480.28
Service agreement	1,595.00
Cash price	34,139.28
DMV fees	.00
State smog fee	6.00
Insurance premiums	.00
Total purchase	34,145.28
Trade-in	.00
Less payoff	.00
Net trade-in	.00
Deferred down	.00
Amount paid now	10,000.00
Total down payment	10,000.00

***** Payment Schedule *****

Due / Starting		Amount
59	12-30-09	543.97
1	11-30-14	543.97

Amount financed	24,145.28
APR	12.56
Finance charge	8,492.92
Total of payments	32,638.20
Total sales price	42,638.20

Consumers need to know this information because the rich people are too greedy and don't really care. Look at where our money is hidden secretly and what we can do to keep the dealers from ripping us off. Friends are telling friends "to get the book."

Computer Printout

Look for extra items to make sure that a service agreement is not smuggled into your monthly payments. Look at the service agreement line below. The amount that is extra is $2,495, added to the customer's monthly payments. This is against the Truth-in Lending Acts. Make sure that you get a copy of the printout.

Price	15,000.00
Accessories	.00
Doc fee	35.00
Sales tax	1,240.39
Service agreement	2,495.00
Cash price	18,770.39

DMV fees	333.00
Insurance premiums	.00
Total purchase	19,103.39

Trade-in	.00
Less payoff	.00
Net trade-in	.00
Deferred down	.00
Amount paid now	5,000.00
Total down payment	5,000.00

***** Payment Schedule *****

Due / Starting		Amount
59	12-30-09	292.76
1	11-30-14	292.76

Amount financed	14,103.39
APR	9.00
Finance charge	3,462.21
Total of payments	17,565.60
Total sales price	22,565.60

Unauthorized funds were taken from many customers. "Thou shall not steal!" And now they are struggling to find customers. They should be honest toward their valuable customer, and their business just might be successful.

Price	15,000.00		
Accessories	.00		
Doc fee	35.00		
Sales tax	1,240.38		
Service agreement	1,595.00		
Cash price	17,870.38		

***** Payment Schedule *****

Due / Starting		Amount
59	12-30-09	357.97
1	11-30-14	357.97

DMV fees	333.00	Amount financed	16,203.38
Insurance premiums	.00	APR	12.51
Total purchase	18,703.38	Finance charge	5,274.82
		Total of payments	21,478.20
		Total sales price	23,478.20

Trade-in	.00
Less payoff	.00
Net trade-in	.00
Deferred down	.00
Amount paid now	2,000.00
Total down payment	2,000.00

Ladies and Gentlemen, have you ever purchased a vehicle from the dealership and later discovered that the contract is much higher than what you were told? Here is a computer printout of $1,595 hidden in the customer's monthly payments. This case is about *Buyers vs. Liars*. This is against the Truth in Lending Acts.

I rest my case!

Price	34,320.20
Accessories	.00
Doc fee	35.00
Dealer smog	.00
Sales tax	2,834.30
Service agreement	2,495.00
Cash price	39,684.50
DMV fees	278.00
Insurance premiums	.00
Total purchase	39,962.50
Trade-in	.00
Less payoff	.00
Net trade-in	.00
Deferred down	.00
Amount paid now	.00
Total down payment	.00

***** Payment Schedule *****

Due / Starting		Amount
59	12-30-09	1,000.00
1	11-30-14	1,000.00

Amount financed	39,962.50
APR	19.9
Finance charges	20,037.50
Total of payments	60,000.00
Total sales price	60,000.00

Answer the question! Did you authorize the dealership to take an extra $2,495 from your pocket and add to your monthly payments before you got to the finance department? Witness:"*No!*" The jury awarded in favor of the Plaintiff.

The dealership's managers who commit fraud by stealing money from the customers with unauthorized approval should be in jail! The customers need the dealers to be honest with them because we are all in this together.

**girls
inc.**

Growing up is
serious business

October 10, 1997

Honda of Oakland
3741 Broadway
Oakland, CA 94611

Dear Phillip,

I would first like to start off by saying that I am very pleased with my car purchase. After my encounter with Cyrus a few weeks ago, I had vowed to give your establishment a very bad name. However, it took a few phone calls from a very sincere gentleman by the name of Darmonica Alexander to change my mind. I felt that Darmonica was genuinely interested in my happiness with regards to any purchasing decisions that I made. He would occasionally phone me to see how I was doing and to discuss the incident that took place with Cyrus. In addition, he invited me to come back to your establishment to discuss the possibility of making a car purchase. At first, I was a bit hesitant due to the bad name Cyrus had given Honda of Oakland and it's staff but I decided to give it one last try. On Tuesday, October 7, 1997, I returned and drove away with my 1997 Honda Civic.

I think you should be very pleased to have someone like Darmonica on your staff. He is definitely an asset to Honda of Oakland. In addition, I would also like to recognize the General Sales Manager, Dave and the Finance Manager, Cynathia Mouton for their professionalism, sincerity, and warmth displayed when handling customers.

Sincerely,

Tiaja Jacks

Chapter 4

Used Car
Official

Guide

Passenger Car

Light-Duty Trucks

CARFAX: WHEN PURCHASING a used vehicle, make sure that you see the Carfax identification number. This is the history of that vehicle. The customer would be able to see if that vehicle had been in an accident, has flood damages or is a salvage title vehicle.

Used Vehicle's Book Value

Example: A customer who wanted to purchase a used vehicle (any vehicle) looked on the Internet, and the Kelly Blue Book value of that vehicle was $13,935. The dealership's asking price was $15,000.00, and the customer had a preapproved loan of 7.9%. The customer wanted to keep the monthly payments at $300. This is the way to beat the dealership at its own game by keeping in mind the $300 monthly payment. The customer must fight for the price, stick to their guns, and make the dealership agree on a deal. Once the dealership agrees with the price, make sure that you get a *computer printout* to see if there are any hidden charges. The buyer ended up paying $13,382.12 by fighting for the price.

Suggested Retail Value (Blue Book)   Condition Excellent Value: $13,935

Price	13,382.12
Accessories	.00
Doc fee	35.00
Sales tax	1,106.91
Service agreement	.00
Cash price	14,524.03
DMV fees	297.00
Insurance premiums	.00
Total purchase	14,821.03

***** Payment Schedule *****

Due / Starting		Amount
59	12-30-09	300.00
1	11-30-14	300.00

Amount financed	14,821.03
APR	7.93
Finance charges	3,178.97
Total of payments	18,000.00
Total sales price	18,000.00

Used Vehicle's Back of Book Value

Excellent Condition Book Value: $7,395.00

Example: A customer wanted to purchase a vehicle for his daughter-in-law to get the grandchildren to and from school. There has been a Kia Optima SE sedan–known as a soft vehicle (not everyone is interested in a Kia). The economy will force consumers to purchase a cheaper vehicle. The dealer's asking price was $8,000.00, but the vehicle had been on the lot for two months. The book value was $7,395.00, and the customer paid $6,658.31. They had a rate of 7.9% from their credit union. The grandparents are now paying $150.00 for 60 months.

Price	6,658.31	******* Payment Schedule *******		
Accessories	.00			
Doc fee	35.00	**Due / Starting**		**Amount**
Sales tax	552.20			
Service agreement	.00	59	12-30-09	150.00
Cash price	7,245.51	1	11-30-14	150.00
DMV fees	165.00	**Amount financed**		7,410.51
Insurance premiums	.00	**APR**		7.93
Total purchase	7,410.51	**Finance charges**		1,589.49
		Total of payments		9,000.00
		Total sales price		9,000.00
Trade-in	.00			
Less payoff	.00			
Net trade-in	.00			
Deferred down	.00			
Amount paid now	.00			
Total down payment				

The Trade-In Vehicle

When the customer has a vehicle to trade in, these are the things he must do in order to get the maximum deal. Bring the trade up after the new vehicle has been negotiated with the seven years and 100,000 miles service agreement with $0 deductible. Then work on trade in vehicle.

Negotiate very hard on the trade-in vehicle and fight for the price as hard as you can. Keep pulling out the trade information that was retrieved from the Internet.

Paying Vehicle Off Early

If a customer wants to pay extra money down with his regular monthly payments, he must indicate that he wants to apply his extra money toward the *principal only*. This must be written on the face of the check. Example: The monthly payments are $450, and the customer wanted to pay an extra $75 per month. When writing his check at $525, note $75 toward principal only. It's about the monthly payments when purchasing a vehicle.

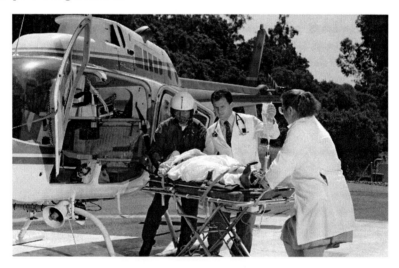

This customer used the *Buyers vs. Liars'* information guidebook and purchased insurance for guaranteed auto protection insurance (GAP) from the finance manager. The vehicle was totaled, and it has been paid off–and their $500 insurance deductible was paid as well. Their old vehicle will show as a paid auto loan on their credit report.

5/1/01

Darmonica Alexander

My name is Ambrosia Knight. I am writing to you on behalf of myself & my fiance Joshua Martinez.

On October 1, 2000, Josh & I bought our first car from Honda of Hayward. A silver 1997 Civic HX 2-door coupe. When we saw that civic for the first time, we both knew what was the car that we wanted to drive home in. Like everyone else, we went through the applications, credit checks, payments, etc. This, of course, brought us to "the finance guy", Darmonica. All we can think is... "More papers?" But we spoke to you about our contract, warranties, & our alarm system.

And this brings me to the point of this letter. We were offered Honda Care, GAP coverage, & an alarm system. These would each add $9 to our monthly payment. We were trying to keep our payments low, thus we were a little reluctant to buy extras. After they were explained, we definitely wanted Honda Care, & our alarm system. We still weren't sure about the GAP coverage, so you explained it more in detail. And we decided we would get it. "Just in case..."

buying it "just in case" came in handy on November 17. Only 1½ months after we bought the car, John was in an accident. He was not hurt, but our Civic was in a ditch on the side of I-80. (Not looking so good.) Two weeks later, our insurance told us that the Civic was totaled. Our insurance did NOT cover the total cost of our financing. There was a substantial difference over the $500 deductible. Luckily, we listened to you about the GAP coverage. That was the best $9 that we've ever spent. It would have cost John & I over $4,000 to finish paying a debt on a car that we weren't even driving.

We just wanted to sincerely thank you for the subtle convincing us to pay $9 more per month, rather than taking the risk of paying a larger amount later. And for the extra time that you have taken from your day to answer our questions & help us when we needed paperwork for our new car. You have always been polite & we'd like you to know that we appreciate it. It means a lot to us because it seems like we're not taken seriously because of our age. You're the only one who was always smiling & always willing to help.

We want you to know that we do tell our friends & family about GAP

coverage & recommend getting it. As a
matter of fact, we have gap coverage on
the car that we just recently bought. Because
we know now that this coverage is worth
every penny. Thank you Again!

Sincerely,

Ambrosia Knight

This payment schedule chart is not just for automobiles. It is for any vehicle. These payment schedule charts can be used for motorcycles, trucks, and jet skis, as well as a nice sports car.

Example: A 1975 convertible had a suggested retail price of $9,995.00 and the customer negotiated and fought for the best price of $8,899.58. With the rate of 7.9% for 60 months, the customer's monthly payments would be $200.00.

Suggested Retail Value $9.995.00

Price	8,899.58		***** Payment Schedule *****	
Accessories	.00			
Doc fee	35.00		Due / Starting	Amount
Sales tax	737.10			
Service agreement	.00		60 12-30-09	200.00
Cash price	9,671.68		1 11-30-14	200.00
DMV fees	209.00		Amount financed	9,880.68
Insurance premiums	.00		APR	7.93
Total purchase	9,880.68		Finance charges	2,119.32
			Total of payments	12,000.00
			Total sales price	12,000.00

Secrets of Payments: Upside Down

If you have a vehicle to trade in, try to keep the trade out of the deal first. Find out about the price on the new vehicle. Let them work out the vehicle purchase price first.

Example: (based on a $20,000 vehicle) is the customer had an SUV and was upside down in his trade. He used the Blue Book to obtain the trade-in value. The dealership's job is to get as much money from you as possible, and the customer's job is to keep as much money in his pocket. The customer called his financial lending institution and asked for a 10-day payoff. Now after finding out that his payoff was **$22,000**, but the book value was **$20,000** (book trade-in value), that means that the customer was upside down **$2,000**. The dealership could only give the customer **$17,000** (net trade-in) for the trade because the gas-guzzler vehicle is not hot on the market anymore. Therefore, the upside-down amount of the customer was **$5,000**. In order to get out of the trade, the customer needed **$5,000** down. See the chart below, where the customer paid the **$5,000** toward the trade-in vehicle. By purchasing the new / used vehicle with this trade-in, it was like putting $0 as a down payment. The customer put another **$5,000** down for the new purchasing vehicle.

Price	20,000.00	***** Payment Schedule *****	
Accessories	.00		
Doc fee	35.00	Due / Starting	Amount
Sales tax	1,652.89		
Service agreement	1,495.00	59 12-30-09	386.44
Cash price	23,182.89	1 11-30-14	386.44
DMV fees	433.00	Amount financed	18,615.89
Insurance premiums	.00	APR	9.00
Total purchase	23,615.89	Finance charges	4,570.51
		Total of payments	23,615.89
		Total sales price	28,615.89
Trade-in	20,000.00		
Less payoff	22,000.00		
Net trade-in	17,000.00		
Deferred down	5,000.00		
Amount paid now	5,000.00		
Total down payment	10,000.00		

There was a total down payment of $10,000, and part of the down payment was for the trade-in vehicle that was upside down.

The American book *Buyers vs. Liars* helped our family in Canada. We saved about $80 monthly on our car payment (savings of $4,800).

This Knowledge Is for Everyone to Know!

This book, *Buyers vs. Liars*, can help people from the United States of America, United Kingdom, Canada and around the world! Are you a buyer or a liar? Knowledge is power, and this book is powerful.

Chapter 5

Leasing Concept

THE LEASING CONCEPT is to be brought up-front with the customer during the qualifying process. Leasing allows the customers to drive the vehicle of their choice, and it's normally for vehicles over $15,000.

This is another way to keep getting money from the customers. If the dealers were honest, they would have repeat customers—that's a fact. When customers are looking at a vehicle of their choice, leasing may be another way that a customer will be able to drive. To lease a vehicle, the customer usually must have a high credit score. If the vehicle is out of your budget, then turn it into a lease. When leasing a vehicle, the insurance is much higher than regular insurance—another add-on payment.

When leasing an automobile, you only pay for the monthly term or the short-usage term. When leasing an automobile, you do not pay for all the taxes in one lump sum; you have monthly taxes. When the dealerships tell you your monthly payment will be $299 per month; they won't ever tell you that you will have the monthly taxes. Now the customer's payment is $326 a month. Now add the higher insurance, and the customer monthly payment is $364.

When purchasing an automobile, one must pay the taxes, title, and license all up-front. While leasing, you must pay a bank fee, security fees, and the first month's payment. There is a drive-off fee. They will say $0 down payment to retain a $199 payment, but there is a drive-off fee. The customer is responsible for all charges. This is similar to a rental vehicle, and the customer must pay for the damages and $.25 per mile over the agreed mile usage (12,000 miles per year).

The residual is the balance of the contract. Example: The price of the vehicle is $25,000, and the residual is $10,000 (remaining balance). This means that the customer is paying $15,000 for the vehicle. This sounds great at first until the customer returns the vehicle to the dealership. I've seen a customer who returned leased vehicles after a four-year lease agreement. If their credit changed for the worse, the customer had to keep the old leased vehicle and then purchase that same vehicle for another 60 months. This was a total of nine years on one vehicle. This is not a good sign. The customer should purchase the vehicle if possible.

If there are damages from a hailstorm, the customer is responsible for all damages. The insurance is much higher on a lease than a purchase. The insurance is about $28+ more than the regular insurance. Once the customer adds up the total monthly payment, they could have purchased the same vehicle for about the same amount of money. Be smart and purchase your next vehicle. All the dealer wants is your money, and that is why what they want you to keep coming back every three years. Purchasing is better for most. Leasing is a waste. What if your leased vehicle were in a flood? Who will pay in the end? the leased customer? That's right.

Lease Return Vehicles or Preowned Vehicles

The lease return vehicle is nothing but a preowned vehicle. Normally, the lease return vehicle has lower miles and regular vehicle service. This is a true story: A customer was returning the lease vehicle with payments of $365 (including tax). Her credit had turned for the worse. The customer went from excellent to bad credit, and she was in need of a vehicle for her family. After three years of leasing that vehicle, she was beyond the required miles that were in her contract and had to pay an extra $450. Her residual was approximately $10,000, which did not include her extra $450 for going over her miles. She loved the leased vehicle, and our sales manager placed her back into her lease return vehicle for another five years of $350 payments with a 19.9% interest rate. This customer has had this vehicle for a total of eight years of monthly payments. Leasing is just to keep the customer coming back time after time with payments. This is a waste of money to me!

This payment chart was the closest to her monthly payments with $12,000.

Price	11,954.42	***** Payment Schedule *****		
Accessories	.00			
Doc fee	35.00	Due / Starting		Amount
Dealer smog	.00			
Sales tax	989.12			
Service agreement	.00	59	12-30-09	350.00
Cash price	12,978.54	1	11-30-14	350.00
DMV fees	132.00	Amount financed		13,110.54
Insurance premiums	.00	APR		19.9
Total purchase	13,110.54	Finance charges		7,889.46
		Total of payments		21,000.00
		Total sales price		21,000.00
Trade-in	.00			
Less payoff	.00			
Net trade-in	.00			
Deferred down	.00			
Amount paid now	.00			
Total down payment	.00			

If you can lease a vehicle because of great credit, use the low rates and purchase it instead. What if you had an accident in your leased vehicle? You or your company is responsible for the damages. This is a waste of money!

Sept 29, 95

To Whom it may Concern:

Darmonica Alexander has splendid salesman skills as well as a very unique approach. He did not just sale me the perfect car. He taught me how to drive it. Which was at least a three and a half hour lesson (5 speed). Mr. Alexander also transported me back and forth to the bank to get a cashiers check to purchase the vehicle. Then to an insurance broker. So, that I was insured. When I drove the car off the Mitsubishi car lot.

I started to have trouble with my car (minor). Yet and still the car was purchased. No longer the dealerships responsibility. Mr. Alexander was not reluctant to come to my aide once again.

Mr. Alexander should be commended for his compassionate demeanor.

Sincerly,

Samara Gardiner

Chapter 6

The Six Secrets Where Your Money Is Stolen!

WHEN A CUSTOMER wants to purchase a vehicle he typically has no clue about the games that the dealership will play to sell him a vehicle. If you have no idea, they will have you purchasing a used vehicle of their choice in order for them to increase their profit. They care less for the soul of a customer and more for the money. It's a matter of the salesperson's thoughts about when he will get another opportunity to get a sucker so uneducated about purchasing a vehicle and earn a bonus commission of $1,400 on one customer.

When the customer is purchasing a vehicle and doesn't know how to fight for the price, he could lose a lot–like $9,000.

The salesperson wants to know how much money you have to put down and what you can afford for a monthly payment. Be aware if you say that you can afford about $300 a month, and can put $3,000 as a down payment. The salesman's job is to make as much money from you as he can. The customer's job should be keeping as much money in his pocket as he can. The salesperson will get you excited about the bonus vehicle, and now you take a test drive. After the salesperson has picked out their vehicle, the salesperson turns in all of the information to the desk manager, and the transaction begins with the closer or assistant sales manager.

They would close the deal by bringing the pencil deal (the offer from the desk), and if the customer goes for the first pencil and agrees for the price of $20,000, rate 9%, payment of $386.44, 60 months term, and a hidden service agreement of $1,495.00, then that's their secret. The customer's payments will be $386.44 a month ($86.44

more than they wanted to pay in the beginning) with *$5,000.00* as a down payment ($2,000.00 more than the original $3,000.00 they were going to put down at first).

Is this Wall Street, or is it the many dealerships all across America? Take your choice. "I promise that this is the best deal, take it or leave it." Leave it and walk out!

Payment schedule chart No. 1 shows where the customer wanted **$300** monthly payments with a **$3,000** down payment. Notice that there is a service agreement of **$1,495** (this is against the Truth-in Lending Acts).

Payment schedule chart No. 2 shows the customer was test-driving the salesperson's bonus vehicle choice, and now the customer's monthly payment is **$386.44** with a **$5,000.00** down payment.

THESE ARE THE SIX "SECRETS of the DEALERSHIPS"

Payment Schedule Chart No. 1

Price	14,409.35
Accessories	.00
Doc fee	35.00
Dealer smog	.00
Sales tax	1,191.66
Service agreement	1,495.00
Cash price	17,131.01
DMV fees	321.00
Insurance premiums	.00
Total purchase	17,452.01
Trade-in	.00
Less payoff	.00
Net trade-in	.00
Deferred down	.00
Amount paid now	3,000.00
Total down payment	3,000.00

***** Payment Schedule *****

Due / Starting		Amount
59	12-30-09	300.00
1	11-30-14	300.00

Amount financed	14,452.01
APR	9.00
Finance charges	3,547.99
Total of payments	18,000.00
Total sales price	21,000.00

****

Payment Schedule Chart No. 2

Price	20,000.00
Accessories	.00
Doc fee	35.00
Dealer smog	.00
Sales tax	1,652.89
Service agreement	1,495.00
Cash price	23,182.89
DMV fees	433.00
Insurance premiums	.00
Total purchase	23,615.89
Trade-in	.00
Less payoff	.00
Net trade-in	.00
Deferred down	.00
Amount paid now	5,000.00
Total down payment	5,000.00

***** Payment Schedule *****

Due / Starting		Amount
59	12-30-09	386.44
1	11-30-14	386.44

Amount financed	18,615.89
APR	9.00
Finance charges	4,570.51
Total of payments	23,186.40
Total sales price	28,186.40

Payment schedule chart No. 3 shows that the customer should have had payments of **$272** a month with **$5,000** as a down payment. Still, they are hiding profits in the service agreement contract of **$1,495**, which is against the Truth-in-Lending Acts. The customers must know exactly what their monthly payments entail.

Payment schedule chart No. 4 shows that the customer should have received a new vehicle with a price of **$15,712.35**, rate of **4.9%** for **48** months, no hidden service agreement of $0.00, monthly payments of **$400.00** with no money ($0.00) as a down payment. If customers are placed in the proper vehicles, they will be able to trade that vehicle in again for their next vehicle; now that's how to get a repeat customer. These are the secrets. This is how the consumer in America can save thousands of dollars.

Here are two final secrets that the dealerships don't want the public to know about buying vehicles. Thanks to *Buyers vs. Liars*, Mom and Dad save extra money for you and me. Now do you want to go to the mall? No, I'd rather save my money for college!

Payment Schedule Chart No. 3

Price	15,000.00
Accessories	.00
Doc fee	35.00
Dealer smog	.00
Sales tax	1,240.39
Service agreement	1,495.00
Cash price	17,770.39
DMV fees	333.00
Insurance premiums	.00
Total purchase	18,103.39
Trade-in	.00
Less payoff	.00
Net trade-in	.00
Deferred down	.00
Amount paid now	5,000.00
Total down payment	5,000.00

***** Payment Schedule *****

Due / Starting		Amount
59	12-30-09	272.00
1	11-30-14	272.00

Amount financed	13,103.39
APR	9.00
Finance charges	3,216.61
Total of payments	16,320.00
Total sales price	21,320.00

****

Payment Schedule Chart No. 4

Price	15,712.35
Accessories	.00
Doc fee	35.00
Dealer smog	.00
Sales tax	1,299.16
Service agreement	.00
Cash price	17,046.51
DMV fees	345.00
Insurance premiums	.00
Total purchase	17,391.51
Trade-in	.00
Less payoff	.00
Net trade-in	.00
Deferred down	.00
Amount paid now	.00
Total down payment	.00

***** Payment Schedule *****

Due / Starting		Amount
47	12-30-09	400.00
1	11-30-13	400.00

Amount financed	17,391.51
APR	4.94
Finance charges	1,808.49
Total of payments	19,200.00
Total sales price	19,200.00

"Look at the Difference"

Chart No. 2 is an example of a customer who doesn't know anything about purchasing a vehicle. The customer's purchase price is $20,000.00 with $5,000.00 as down payment, <u>*9.0%*</u> rates and a monthly payment of $386.44 for five years. The total purchase price of this contract is $28,186.40. Note that 9.0% is good credit.

Chart No. 4 is an example of a customer who used this information and guidebook. This customer's purchase price is $15,712.35 with $0.00 as a down payment, 4.95% rate, and 48 monthly payments of $400.00. The total purchase price of this contract is $19,200.00. Note also, to qualify for a 4.9% rate, your credit score must be good!

The difference from chart No. 2 and chart No. 4 is $8,986.40 worth of savings when the customer knows the total picture regarding purchasing a vehicle. *Buyers vs. Liars* will help the American citizens by saving his families more money when they purchase vehicles in the future. This information book is about saving money! This is how the public will not get ripped off!
1. Price/Down, 2. Rate, 3. Term, 4. Service Agreement, 5. Payment and 6. Leasing

Payment Schedule Chart No. 2

Price	20,000.00
Accessories	.00
Doc fee	35.00
Dealer smog	.00
Sales tax	1,652.89
Service agreement	1,495.00
Cash price	23,182.89
DMV fees	433.00
Insurance premiums	.00
Total purchase	23,615.89
Trade-in	.00
Less payoff	.00
Net trade-in	.00
Deferred down	.00
Amount paid now	5,000.00
Total down payment	5,000.00

***** Payment Schedule *****

Due / Starting		Amount
59	12-30-09	386.44
1	11-30-14	386.44

Amount financed	18,615.89
APR	9.00
Finance charges	4,570.51
Total of payments	23,186.40
Total sales price	28,186.40

****

Payment Schedule Chart No. 4

Price	15,712.35
Accessories	.00
Doc fee	35.00
Dealer smog	.00
Sales tax	1,299.16
Service agreement	.00
Cash price	17,046.51
DMV fees	345.00
Insurance premiums	.00
Total purchase	17,391.51
Trade-in	.00
Less payoff	.00
Net trade-in	.00
Deferred down	.00
Amount paid now	.00
Total down payment	.00

***** Payment Schedule *****

Due / Starting		Amount
47	12-30-09	400.00
1	11-30-13	400.00

Amount financed	17,391.51
APR	4.9
Finance charges	1,808.49
Total of payments	19,200.00
Total sales price	19,200.00

May 18, 1999

Ellen Schweitzer
859 Warfield Ave. #12
Oakland, CA 94610

Philip Mah, Manager
Honda Oakland
3741 Broadway
Oakland, CA 94611

Dear Mr. Mah:

I am writing in behalf of your employee, Darmonica Alexander. I have been a patron of Oakland Honda since 1992 and get all my service done there. In all of those years, I have never received such good service from an employee as I did from Mr. Alexander. He went above and beyond the call of duty to help me with a problem I was having with my Honda. I didn't even have an appointment and usually people there are so busy that there is little time to help a drop-in customer with a minor problem.

Mr. Alexander went out of his way to help take care of me. He was courteous, kind, helpful and sincere about helping me.

Please see to it that Mr. Alexander is sufficiently rewarded in some way for his excellent customer service. I really did appreciate it.

Thank you.

Sincerely,

Ellen Schweitzer

Chapter 7

Conclusion

REMEMBER THESE STEPS when purchasing a vehicle. Don't go to the dealership and think that you can just talk to a salesperson and think that you are going to come out alive; they will eat you alive, and you will not know what happened until you come from the ether (chemistry liquid solvent and anesthetic; a voltaic colorless liquid with a pleasant smell used as a solvent and formerly used as an anesthetic). Don't be dumb!

Things To Do

*   Shop at night when the dealership is closed. Select a few vehicles, go online, and look up the vehicle of your choice and compare.
*   If possible, get a preapproved loan with the credit union's interest rates and fight for the price with this book and information guide.
*   Go back to the dealership, select the vehicle of your choice, take a test drive, then you can work on the dealer's nerves for a change. Now the buyer has the buying power. Don't fall for the monthly payment game unless you have the *Buyers vs. Liars* information guidebook. Then you can beat them at their own game.
*   Once you have agreed on the monthly terms, demand to see a payment chart. If they refuse to let you see it, stand up and walk out. They will come running for your business. Look at the payment schedule chart to see if they have smuggled in any extra goodies without your authorization.

* Before you enter the finance department, negotiate the price and request for seven years and 100,000 miles with a $0 deductible. The cost is around $800. Ask to see their cost. Now that this book is out, some dealers just make up a fake or a dummy price sheet. You may give $100 over cost. Remember, they *need* to earn a little commission on the back end. Get a package and negotiate with the finance manager.

* If you are getting a used vehicle with interest rates 7% or higher, please ask your credit union or dealership for a GAP (guaranteed auto protection insurance) insurance policy that will cover your vehicle interest rate and pay for your deductible if your vehicle is totaled. See your credit union, bank, or dealer for more details.

Do not add a lot of extra items to your monthly payments; save some cash to pay for some extra items in the finance department. If you add extra accessories to your monthly payment, then you are giving away more money than you think in financing. Make sure that you have GAP insurance added to the vehicle. It's funny how the dealers have ripped off many customers, and now their doors are being closed down. *God* don't like *ugly*! If they were honest, who knows what would have happened. *Remember to fight for the price.*

Once you have followed the six secrets of the auto dealerships and are satisfied with monthly payments up-front with the sales manager, before you go into the finance department make sure that you have your seven years and 100,000 miles with $0 deductible warranty. Do not take the sales manager's word. They are big liars. The customer must make sure that their warranty is added into their monthly payments before they enter into the finance department or no deal.

Once you get into the finance department, this is where you should spend your money for accessories. This is where you should purchase the maximum package (don't get a package if it's not affordable) with the finance manager. Get the paint and fabric seal, alarm system, tinted windows, DVD system and GAP insurance, especially if you have an interest rate over 7%. The finance manager who works with you can help you save more money, but he or she also helps you get the best and honest financing. It will be worth every penny. Get to know your finance manager for the next 60 days. That way, the manager will remember you as a valued customer. The dealer may make less money, but repeat customers will keep the dealer's door open forever by being honest and fair.

Your finance manager should explain to you in detail about your contract and your accessories. Remember, the more cover that you put in the purchase department, the better off, but don't go overboard. This is the time to spend for extra protection in cash!

THIS WILL BE ONE OF MY VICE-PRESIDENT/PARTNERS AND PROMOTERS—"HELEN RAMOS" DREAM BOAT." SHE DESERVES THE BEST.

Bankruptcy . . . APPROVED!
Repossessions . . . APPROVED!
Foreclosure . . . APPROVED!

Watch out for the dealership advertising!

You are approved for the highest monthly payments. You are approved for the highest percentage rates. You are approved for the highest warranty with less coverage.

You are approved for the highest monthly payments. You are approved with more down payments–two weeks later, we need some more money for your down payment.

Now dealerships will be offering everything that they can just to get you in the door. They must pay for their "Bailout" loan back to the U.S. government, and who do you think that they are going to get all of that "Bailout" money from? You! They are going to try to deceive the customer and charge way more than normal. Will a dealership rob a customer'? Yet ye have robbed them, but ye say, wherein have we robbed thee? For where will a dealership rob a customer, through warranties and high prices on vehicle or through navigation system or leasing.

Will there be another one?

Thanks to "Buyers vs. Liars "information book guide, this will allow millions of valuable customers to "know before they go."

September 7, 1995

To: Darmonica Alexander

Subject: Performance

On June 17, 1995 Clarence J. Dominguez Jr purchased a 1995 Mitsubishi Mirage, On June 24, 1995 his sister Carmen Reese purchased a 1995 Mitsubishi Mirage, their father Clarence Dominguez Sr. Purchased an automobile in 7/95, all of the automobiles were bought from Weatherford Mitsubishi and Darmonica Alexander was the salesperson.

Because of Darmonica Alexander's superb performance, personality, and exempliary courtesy, it was easy for the family to continue going to this dealership and requesting his assistance.

Because of the time of day, Carmen's car was not cleaned before it left the premises. Darmonica went to Carmen's place of employment to picked up her car for cleaning and returned it, due to Carmen's extended work hours she was unable to do this herself.

Darmonica exemplified customer service to it's fullest.

Sincerely,

Clarence J. Dominguez Jr.

Carmen C. Reese

Clarence J. Dominguez Sr.

John R. Noche
RMN ENTERPRISES
Post Office Box 693113
Stockton, CA 95210
(209) 473-7357

February 23, 1993

Mr. Bud Norris,
Jeep Sales Manager
SMITH JEEP/EAGLE
12380 San Pablo Avenue
Richmond, CA 94805

Dear Mr. Norris:

I purchased a Grand Cherokee earlier this month at your dealership, and I would like you to know that it has been very enjoyable driving it.

The friendly service that we received at your dealership was very welcomed after spending most of our day in the Bay Area quite disappointed with the service we received at other auto dealers. Darmonica Alexander was very helpful, and I might add, very patient during the four hours it took us to finally close a deal to our satisfaction. It is nice to know that you can still get no-pressure service from an automobile dealership.

Thank you for your professional help in our investment decision.

Very truly yours,

RMN ENTERPRISES

John R. Noche
President

JRN:cv

405 Rancho Arroyo Pkwy. #305
Fremont, CA 94536
February 23, 1996

Mr. Thomas O'Leary
Hayward Ford
25501 Mission Blvd.
Hayward, CA 94544

Dear Mr. O'Leary:

I was impressed with your dealership from the moment I arrived. The selection was incredible. The lot was clean. But to be honest with you, I had no intention of purchasing a vehicle for another 11 months. A member of your sales staff, Darmonica Alexander, played a significant part in my decision to "take the big step".

Darmonica was friendly and professional. He has a sales style that I was very comfortable with. No pressure. No "B.S.". In fact, I was only looking on that afternoon. Darmonica convinced me to take a new Ranger for a test drive. That was all it took. I knew the Ranger was the right truck for me. I now drive a 1996 Ford Ranger truck that I purchased (leased) at your dealership.

Please extend my thanks and appreciation to Darmonica Alexander for a job well done. Also, thank you for taking the time (a long time) to explain the "ins and outs" of leasing. If you have any questions for me or need any additional information, please don't hesitate to ask. I can be reached anytime at (510) 659 - 5766. Thank you.

Sincerely,

Forest J. Keener, ATCS
Federal Aviation Administration

Tom O'Leary   March 17, 1996
Sales Manager
Hayward Ford
25501 Mission Blvd.
Hayward, Ca. 94544

Re: Pleased with recent purchase

Dear Mr. O'Leary,
On March 12, 1996 my wife and I bought a new 1997 Ford F-150 pick-up.
Our sales representative was Darmonica Alexander. I have never
purchased a new vehicle from your place of business before. However,
the experience is to be commended. Over the years I've bought several
new cars and trucks from other dealerships in the area. Let me just say
this, "they don't even come close to the courtesy or hassle free car
shopping your business does". We were both pleased with Darmonica s'
honesty and knowledge of your products.

Since we purchased our new Ford truck we have been passing along to
friends and family the message " the place to buy new or used vehicles is
Hayward Ford". We look forward to using your parts and service
departments to see if they meet the same customer satisfaction we
received the day we bought our vehicle. Thank you.

                              Sincerely,

                              Michael & Stacy DeGrano
                              Michael and Stacy DeGrano

April 6, 1995

Weatherford Mitsubishi
750 Potter Street
Berkeley, CA 94710

To Whom It May Concern:

On Saturday, February 4, 1995, I was on my way to Weatherford BMW to purchase a car.

While walking past the Mitsubishi dealership, I noticed a pleasant-looking gentleman standing out front. He said to me and a friend, "we have some excellent deals - won't you come have a look?" ·

I told him that I was looking for a BMW, but that I would stop by later to check out the Mitsubishi's. (Being a former Mitsubishi owner, I knew that they were good performance cars.)

The gentleman told me that I should check out the Mitsubishis because they were having a "weekend blowout" on '94 cars. My cousin and I took his suggestion.

He introduced himself as Darmonica Alexander. We walked around the showroom and lot. The 3000GT caught my eye and I asked to test drive it. He pulled the car around, and after explaining all the features, we were off.

Upon approaching the freeway, I realized that there was very little gas left in the tank, so we returned to the dealership. I requested that the tank be filled, and the radio be programmed in order to check out the sound system. Mr. Alexander kindly obliged me and again, we were off to test drive the car.

After driving for about an hour - I fell in love. Upon my return, I was certain that I would not leave without this car.

I had a 1971 220D Mercedes and about $500.00 for a down payment on a $26,000+ car. In addition, I told him that I did not my monthly payment to exceed $400.00 a month. He worked with me (and the finance department) for over an hour.

My experience in dealing with **Mr. Alexander was professional, pleasant, humorous and most delightful.** We finally reached a d**u**able deal.

Upon signing all of the necessary documents, he made sure that all of my questions concerning the car were answered. I had to return the following week to have my burglar alarm installed. I left the car, and he later called me when it was ready.

When I left the lot at the date of purchase, Mr. Alexander told me that if I had any questions, problems or concerns to feel free to contact him. And I did. Any little question that creeped into my brain - I would ask him. He was always very attentive, and would refer me to whomever could help me.

It is obvious to me that Mr. Alexander has a genuine concern for his customers. I feel he is a wonderful asset to Weatherford, and he makes buying a new car very exciting due to his great interpersonal skills and personality.

Darmonica, thanks again for all of your assistance!

Sincerely,

Deirdre A. Williams

July 10. 1996

Barney Barnblatt
Hayward Ford
25501 Mission Blvd.
Hayward, CA. 94544

Barney, I want to formally thank you and your staff for the exceptional service I received today when purchasing my 1996 Ford Ranger.

There are many factors that are important to a customer when making a major purchase like this and you guys didn't overlook any detail in making me feel good about the entire transaction.

It started with a phone call to you explaining my interest and needs. You immediately made me feel comfortable that you would be working to help me. When I arrived at the lot I was quickly introduced to Darmonica Alexander who greeted me with courtesy and sincerity.

Darmonica demonstrated great knowledge of his product and a great deal of patience in helping me find the truck to fit my needs. Once we found the Ranger that I was interested in he convinced me that he would work to make the deal a reality, and he did. Darmonica is a great salesperson!

Also. I would like to send a special thanks to Tom O'Dea for his professional and respectful communication with me during the final transaction.

I haven't bought an American vehicle in about twenty years. but with this kind of service I just might make it a habit.

Yours truly.

Ken Gibson
Manager. Engine Maintenance
United Airlines

cc: Darmonica Alexander✓
    Tom O'Dea

601 Van Ness Ave. #621
San Francisco, CA 94102
September 23, 1993

Mr. E. T. Pappert
Vice President, Sales
Chrysler Corporation
P. O. Box 5022
Rochester, Michigan 48308-9973

Dear Mr. Pappert:

My wife and I recently purchased a 1993 Jeep Grand Cherokee Limited from Smith Chrysler/Plymouth/Jeep/Eagle located at 12380 San Pablo Avenue in Richmond, California. We are both very happy with the Jeep Grand Cherokee. It's a well engineered, quality vehicle with many outstanding features that truly make it a pleasure to drive.

My wife and I were also pleased with all of the people at the Smith Jeep/Eagle dealership, and especially with our salesperson, Mr. Darmonica Alexander. From the first time I met Darmonica, I had the feeling that he was an honest person who was sincerely interested in me as a customer. He went out of his way to answer all of our questions, listened to what we wanted (or thought we wanted), and most importantly helped us get a good price. In addition, Darmonica personally took time after the sale to help me select and purchase a new ski rack at the Smith Jeep/Eagle Parts Department, which I greatly appreciated.

Many thanks for Chrysler's commitment in making such a fine vehicle, and also for the great service that we received from everyone at Smith Jeep/Eagle.

Sincerely yours,

Thomas B. Colbourn

Thomas B. Colbourn

cc: Mr. Bud Norris, Smith Jeep/Eagle

Mr. Darmonica Alexander, Smith Jeep/Eagle

November 11, 1993

Congratulations!

This **Gold Weekend Select** award entitles you to a wonderful weekend escape — one night of fun and relaxation at many Marriott locations across the Continental United States, with a complimentary breakfast for two the next morning. You'll enjoy Marriott's exceptional service on Friday, Saturday, or Sunday night.

Participating locations are on the back of this letter. Advance reservations are required. Call 1-800-228-9290 to make your reservations (please refer to #2 under Terms and conditions on the back of this certificate) and be sure to present your award when you check in.

We look forward to welcoming you soon.

Mystery Shopper
Award 11-21-93

S.F. Auto Show

Sincerely,

Steve Weisz
Senior Vice President
Sales & Marketing

CA JEEP/EAGLE DAA
20253-B Redwood Road
Castro Valley, CA 94546

previously paid for this award.
are non-commissionable.

The consumers are looking for dishonest dealerships. This will save billions of dollars for the consumers. *Buyers vs. Liars,* get it! The secret is out!

Not-So-Special Financing

There are some large auto dealer groups charging customers with poor credit 32% instead o f 19% or 21% rates. They are telling the customers that they have to send their contracts to the state of Nevada to get them approved. They are just making their customers pay more because they are in need of a vehicle very badly. This is still against the Truth-in Lending Acts and there should be an investigation against those dealerships.

Chapter 8

THE FOLLOWING PAYMENT schedule chart is divided into short-term monthly payments, such as 24 months at 2.9% interest rates, 36 months at 3.9% interest rates, and 48 months at 4.9%. After you have decided the length of term, 24 to 48 months, locate the monthly payment that you can afford.

Once the payment has been determined, look at the payment schedule chart and then look at the price of the vehicle that will allow you to see what you are getting into. Example:

		***** Payment Schedule *****	
Price	13,741.04		
Accessories	.00		
Doc fee	35.00	Due / Starting	Amount
Sales tax	1,136.52		
Service agreement	.00	47 12-30-09	350.00
Cash price	14,912.36	1 11-30-13	350.00
DMV fees	305.00	Amount financed	15,217.56
Insurance premiums	.00	APR	4.94
Total purchase	15,217.56	Finance charges	1,582.44
		Total of payments	16,800.00
		Total sales price	16,800.00
Trade-in	.00		
Less payoff	.00		
Net trade-in	.00		
Deferred down	.00		
Amount paid now	.00		
Total down payment	.00		

The MSRP is $15,105. Negotiate on your monthly payment budget with the dealer and stay with your budget. This way, it allows the buyer to have the upper hand on the monthly payment. The only way to meet your payments is to reduce the price of the vehicle or the percentage rates or both.

To find your budget payment, calculate your family budget such as $350.00 a month. Next, find your approved rates, such as 4.9% for 48 months.

1. There is a choice of 24 months for two years, 36 months for three years, 48 months for four years, and 60 months for five years. The majority of customers use 60 months. Try to stay with five years for 60 months. It's very important to know your interest rates before going to the dealer. This is where they will rip you off! Get a preapproved loan.

2. Turn to the back of *Buyers vs. Liars* and locate 48 months, next locate your payments at $350.00.

3. Now your MSRP price of $15,105 has reduced to $13,741.00. If your budget is $350.00 a month, tell the dealer your payments are $325.00, just to make them feel good.

At a young age, we are going to keep our eye on our finances!
Next, we are going to *change* our old ways.

This chapter contents short term monthly payments, such as 24, 36, and 48 month payments.

Payment Schedule Charts at 2.95% for 24 Months

Price	2,048.04
Accessories	.00
Doc fee	35.00
Sales tax	171.85
Service agreement	.00
Cash price	2,254.89

***** Payment Schedule *****

Due / Starting		Amount
23	12-30-09	100.00
1	11-30-11	100.00

DMV fees	73.00
Insurance premiums	.00
Total purchase	2,327.89

Amount financed	2,327.89
APR	2.95
Finance charges	72.11
Total of payments	2,400.00
Total sales price	2,400.00

Trade-in	.00
Less payoff	.00
Net trade-in	.00
Deferred down	.00
Amount paid now	.00
Total down payment	.00

****

Price	3,104.81
Accessories	.00
Doc fee	35.00
Sales tax	259.03
Service agreement	.00
Cash price	3,398.84

***** Payment Schedule *****

Due / Starting		Amount
23	12-30-09	150.00
1	11-30-11	150.00

DMV fees	93.00
Insurance premiums	.00
Total purchase	3,491.84

Amount financed	3,491.84
APR	2.95
Finance charges	108.16
Total of payments	3,600.00
Total sales price	3,600.00

Trade-in	.00
Less payoff	.00
Net trade-in	.00
Deferred down	.00
Amount paid now	.00
Total down payment	.00

Price	4,161.58
Accessories	.00
Doc fee	35.00
Sales tax	346.22
Service agreement	.00
Cash price	4,542.80

DMV fees	113.00
Insurance premiums	.00
Total purchase	4,655.80

Trade-in	.00
Less payoff	.00
Net trade-in	.00
Deferred down	.00
Amount paid now	.00
Total down payment	.00

***** Payment Schedule *****

Due / Starting		Amount
23	12-30-09	200.00
1	11-30-11	200.00

Amount financed	4,655.80
APR	2.95
Finance charges	144.20
Total of payments	4,800.00
Total sales price	4,800.00

****

Price	5,214.65
Accessories	.00
Doc fee	35.00
Sales tax	433.10
Service agreement	.00
Cash price	5,682.75

DMV fees	137.00
Insurance premiums	.00
Total purchase	5,819.75

Trade-in	.00
Less payoff	.00
Net trade-in	.00
Deferred down	.00
Amount paid now	.00
Total down payment	.00

***** Payment Schedule *****

Due / Starting		Amount
23	12-30-09	250.00
1	11-30-11	250.00

Amount financed	5,819.75
APR	2.95
Finance charges	180.25
Total of payments	6,000.00
Total sales price	6,000.00

Price	6,271.41
Accessories	.00
Doc fee	35.00
Sales tax	520.28
Service agreement	.00
Cash price	6,826.69
DMV fees	157.00
Insurance premiums	.00
Total purchase	6,983.69
Trade-in	.00
Less payoff	.00
Net trade-in	.00
Deferred down	.00
Amount paid now	.00
Total down payment	.00

***** Payment Schedule *****

Due / Starting		Amount
23	12-30-09	300.00
1	11-30-11	300.00

Amount financed	6,983.69
APR	2.95
Finance charges	216.31
Total of payments	7,200.00
Total sales price	7,200.00

****

Price	7,328.18
Accessories	.00
Doc fee	35.00
Sales tax	607.46
Service agreement	.00
Cash price	7,970.64
DMV fees	177.00
Insurance premiums	.00
Total purchase	8,147.64
Trade-in	.00
Less payoff	.00
Net trade-in	.00
Deferred down	.00
Amount paid now	.00
Total down payment	.00

***** Payment Schedule *****

Due / Starting		Amount
23	12-30-09	350.00
1	11-30-11	350.00

Amount financed	8,147.64
APR	2.95
Financecharges	252.36
Total of payments	8,400.00
Total sales price	8,400.00

Price	8,384.95
Accessories	.00
Doc fee	35.00
Sales tax	694.65
Service agreement	.00
Cash price	9,114.60

DMV fees	197.00
Insurance premiums	.00
Total purchase	9,311.60

Trade-in	.00
Less payoff	.00
Net trade-in	.00
Deferred down	.00
Amount paid now	.00
Total down payment	.00

***** Payment Schedule *****

Due / Starting		Amount
23	12-30-09	400.00
1	11-30-11	400.00

Amount financed	9,311.60
APR	2.95
Finance charges	288.40
Total of payments	9,600.00
Total sales price	9,600.00

****

Price	9,438.02
Accessories	.00
Doc fee	35.00
Sales tax	781.52
Service agreement	.00
Cash price	10,254.54

DMV fees	221.00
Insurance premiums	.00
Total purchase	10,475.54

Trade-in	.00
Less payoff	.00
Net trade-in	.00
Deferred down	.00
Amount paid now	.00
Total down payment	.00

***** Payment Schedule *****

Due / Starting		Amount
23	12-30-09	450.00
1	11-30-11	450.00

Amount financed	10,475.54
APR	2.95
Finance charges	324.46
Total of payments	10,800.00
Total sales price	10,800.00

Price	10,494.78
Accessories	.00
Doc fee	35.00
Sales tax	868.71
Service agreement	.00
Cash price	11,398.49
DMV fees	241.00
Insurance premiums	.00
Total purchase	11,639.49
Trade-in	.00
Less payoff	.00
Net trade-in	.00
Deferred down	.00
Amount paid now	.00
Total down payment	.00

***** Payment Schedule *****

Due / Starting		Amount
23	12-30-09	500.00
1	11-30-11	500.00

Amount financed	11,639.49
APR	2.95
Finance charges	360.51
Total of payments	12,000.00
Total sales price	12,000.00

****

Price	11,551.55
Accessories	.00
Doc fee	35.00
Sales tax	955.89
Service agreement	.00
Cash price	12,542.44
DMV fees	261.00
Insurance premiums	.00
Total purchase	12,803.44
Trade-in	.00
Less payoff	.00
Net trade-in	.00
Deferred down	.00
Amount paid now	.00
Total down payment	.00

***** Payment Schedule *****

Due / Starting		Amount
23	12-30-09	550.00
1	11-30-11	550.00

Amount financed	12,803.44
APR	2.95
Finance charges	396.56
Total of payments	13,200.00
Total sales price	13,200.00

Price	12,604.62
Accessories	.00
Doc fee	35.00
Sales tax	1,042.77
Service agreement	.00
Cash price	13,682.39

DMV fees	285.00
Insurance premiums	.00
Total purchase	13,967.39

Trade-in	.00
Less payoff	.00
Net trade-in	.00
Deferred down	.00
Amount paid now	.00
Total down payment	.00

***** Payment Schedule *****

Due / Starting		Amount
23	12-30-09	600.00
1	11-30-11	600.00

Amount financed	13,967.39
APR	2.95
Finance charges	432.61
Total of payments	14,400.00
Total sales price	14,400.00

****

Price	13,661.39
Accessories	.00
Doc fee	35.00
Sales tax	1,129.95
Service agreement	.00
Cash price	14,826.34

DMV fees	305.00
Insurance premiums	.00
Total purchase	15,131.34

Trade-in	.00
Less payoff	.00
Net trade-in	.00
Deferred down	.00
Amount paid now	.00
Total down payment	.00

***** Payment Schedule *****

Due / Starting		Amount
23	12-30-09	650.00
1	11-30-11	650.00

Amount financed	15,131.34
APR	2.95
Finance charges	468.66
Total of payments	15,600.00
Total sales price	15,600.00

Price	14,718.15
Accessories	.00
Doc fee	35.00
Sales tax	1,217.13
Service agreement	.00
Cash price	15,970.28

DMV fees	325.00
Insurance premiums	.00
Total purchase	16,295.28

Trade-in	.00
Less payoff	.00
Net trade-in	.00
Deferred down	.00
Amount paid now	.00
Total down payment	.00

***** Payment Schedule *****

Due / Starting		Amount
23	12-30-09	700.00
1	11-30-11	700.00

Amount financed	16,295.28
APR	2.95
Finance charges	504.72
Total of payments	16,800.00
Total sales price	16,800.00

****

Price	15,774.92
Accessories	.00
Doc fee	35.00
Sales tax	1,304.32
Service agreement	.00
Cash price	17,114.24

DMV fees	345.00
Insurance premiums	.00
Total purchase	17,459.24

Trade-in	.00
Less payoff	.00
Net trade-in	.00
Deferred down	.00
Amount paid now	.00
Total down payment	.00

***** Payment Schedule *****

Due / Starting		Amount
23	12-30-09	750.00
1	11-30-11	750.00

Amount financed	17,459.24
APR	2.95
Finance charges	540.76
Total of payments	18,000.00
Total sales price	18,000.00

Price	16,827.99
Accessories	.00
Doc fee	35.00
Sales tax	1,391.20
Service agreement	.00
Cash price	18,254.19

DMV fees	369.00
Insurance premiums	.00
Total purchase	18,623.19

Trade-in	.00
Less payoff	.00
Net trade-in	.00
Deferred down	.00
Amount paid now	.00
Total down payment	.00

***** Payment Schedule *****

Due / Starting		Amount
23	12-30-09	800.00
1	11-30-11	800.00

Amount financed	18,623.19
APR	2.95
Finance charges	576.81
Total of payments	19,200.00
Total sales price	19,200.00

****

Price	17,884.75
Accessories	.00
Doc fee	35.00
Sales tax	1,478.38
Service agreement	.00
Cash price	19,398.13

DMV fees	389.00
Insurance premiums	.00
Total purchase	19,787.13

Trade-in	.00
Less payoff	.00
Net trade-in	.00
Deferred down	.00
Amount paid now	.00
Total down payment	.00

***** Payment Schedule *****

Due / Starting		Amount
23	12-30-09	850.00
1	11-30-11	850.00

Amount financed	19,787.13
APR	2.95
Finance charges	612.87
Total of payments	20,400.00
Total sales price	20,400.00

Price	18,941.52
Accessories	.00
Doc fee	35.00
Sales tax	1,565.56
Service agreement	.00
Cash price	20,542.08

DMV fees	409.00
Insurance premiums	.00
Total purchase	20,951.08

Trade-in	.00
Less payoff	.00
Net trade-in	.00
Deferred down	.00
Amount paid now	.00
Total down payment	.00

***** Payment Schedule *****

Due / Starting		Amount
23	12-30-09	900.00
1	11-30-11	900.00

Amount financed	20,951.08
APR	2.95
Finance charges	648.92
Total of payments	21,600.00
Total sales price	21,600.00

****

Price	19,998.29
Accessories	.00
Doc fee	35.00
Sales tax	1,652.75
Service agreement	.00
Cash price	21,686.04

DMV fees	429.00
Insurance premiums	.00
Total purchase	22,115.04

Trade-in	.00
Less payoff	.00
Net trade-in	.00
Deferred down	.00
Amount paid now	.00
Total down payment	.00

***** Payment Schedule *****

Due / Starting		Amount
23	12-30-09	950.00
1	11-30-11	950.00

Amount financed	22,115.04
APR	2.95
Finance charges	684.96
Total of payments	22,800.00
Total sales price	22,800.00

Price	21,051.36	***** Payment Schedule *****	
Accessories	.00		
Doc fee	35.00	**Due / Starting**	**Amount**
Sales tax	1,739.62		
Service agreement	.00	23 12-30-09	1,000.00
Cash price	22,825.98	1 11-30-11	1,000.00
DMV fees	453.00	Amount financed	23,278.98
Insurance premiums	.00	APR	2.95
Total purchase	23,278.98	Finance charges	721.02
		Total of payments	24,000.00
		Total sales price	24,000.00
Trade-in	.00		
Less payoff	.00		
Net trade-in	.00		
Deferred down	.00		
Amount paid now	.00		
Total down payment	.00		

****

To balance our family budget, we used *Buyers vs. Liars* and saved money on our transportation.

Payment Schedule Charts at 3.99%
for 36 Months

			***** Payment Schedule *****	
Price	3,008.49			
Accessories	.00			
Doc fee	35.00		**Due / Starting**	**Amount**
Sales tax	251.09			
Service agreement	.00		35 12-30-09	100.00
Cash price	3,294.58		1 11-30-12	100.00
DMV fees	93.00		Amount financed	3,387.58
Insurance premiums	.00		APR	3.99
Total purchase	3,387.58		Finance charges	212.42
			Total of payments	3,600.00
			Total sales price	3,600.00
Trade-in	.00			
Less payoff	.00			
Net trade-in	.00			
Deferred down	.00			
Amount paid now	.00			
Total down payment	.00			

****

			***** Payment Schedule *****	
Price	4,547.33			
Accessories	.00			
Doc fee	35.00		**Due / Starting**	**Amount**
Sales tax	378.04			
Service agreement	.00		35 12-30-09	150.00
Cash price	4,960.37		1 11-30-12	150.00
DMV fees	121.00		Amount financed	5,081.37
Insurance premiums	.00		APR	3.99
Total purchase	5,081.37		Finance charges	318.63
			Total of payments	5,400.00
			Total sales price	5,400.00
Trade-in	.00			
Less payoff	.00			
Net trade-in	.00			
Deferred down	.00			
Amount paid now	.00			
Total down payment	.00			

Price	6,082.47
Accessories	.00
Doc fee	35.00
Sales tax	504.69
Service agreement	.00
Cash price	6,622.16
DMV fees	153.00
Insurance premiums	.00
Total purchase	6,775.16
Trade-in	.00
Less payoff	.00
Net trade-in	.00
Deferred down	.00
Amount paid now	.00
Total down payment	.00

***** Payment Schedule *****

Due / Starting		Amount
35	12-30-09	200.00
1	11-30-12	200.00

Amount financed	6,775.16
APR	3.99
Finance charges	424.84
Total of payments	7,200.00
Total sales price	7,200.00

****

Price	7,617.61
Accessories	.00
Doc fee	35.00
Sales tax	631.34
Service agreement	.00
Cash price	8,283.95
DMV fees	185.00
Insurance premiums	.00
Total purchase	8,468.95
Trade-in	.00
Less payoff	.00
Net trade-in	.00
Deferred down	.00
Amount paid now	.00
Total down payment	.00

***** Payment Schedule *****

Due / Starting		Amount
35	12-30-09	250.00
1	11-30-12	250.00

Amount financed	8,468.95
APR	3.99
Finance charges	531.05
Total of payments	9,000.00
Total sales price	9,000.00

Price	9,156.44
Accessories	.00
Doc fee	35.00
Sales tax	758.29
Service agreement	.00
Cash price	9,949.73
DMV fees	213.00
Insurance premiums	.00
Total purchase	10,162.73
Trade-in	.00
Less payoff	.00
Net trade-in	.00
Deferred down	.00
Amount paid now	.00
Total down payment	.00

***** Payment Schedule *****

Due / Starting		Amount
35	12-30-09	300.00
1	11-30-12	300.00

Amount financed	10,162.73
APR	3.99
Finance charges	637.27
Total of payments	10,800.00
Total sales price	10,800.00

****

Price	10,691.59
Accessories	.00
Doc fee	35.00
Sales tax	884.94
Service agreement	.00
Cash price	11,611.53
DMV fees	245.00
Insurance premiums	.00
Total purchase	11,856.53
Trade-in	.00
Less payoff	.00
Net trade-in	.00
Deferred down	.00
Amount paid now	.00
Total down payment	.00

***** Payment Schedule *****

Due / Starting		Amount
35	12-30-09	350.00
1	11-30-12	350.00

Amount financed	11,856.53
APR	3.99
Finance charges	743.47
Total of payments	12,600.00
Total sales price	12,600.00

Price	12,226.73
Accessories	.00
Doc fee	35.00
Sales tax	1,011.59
Service agreement	.00
Cash price	13,273.32
DMV fees	277.00
Insurance premiums	.00
Total purchase	13,550.32
Trade-in	.00
Less payoff	.00
Net trade-in	.00
Deferred down	.00
Amount paid now	.00
Total down payment	.00

***** Payment Schedule *****

Due / Starting		Amount
35	12-30-09	400.00
1	11-30-12	400.00

Amount financed	13,550.32
APR	3.99
Finance charges	849.68
Total of payments	14,400.00
Total sales price	14,400.00

****

Price	13,765.56
Accessories	.00
Doc fee	35.00
Sales tax	1,138.55
Service agreement	.00
Cash price	14,939.11
DMV fees	305.00
Insurance premiums	.00
Total purchase	15,244.11
Trade-in	.00
Less payoff	.00
Net trade-in	.00
Deferred down	.00
Amount paid now	.00
Total down payment	.00

***** Payment Schedule *****

Due / Starting		Amount
35	12-30-09	450.00
1	11-30-12	450.00

Amount financed	15,244.11
APR	3.99
Finance charges	955.89
Total of payments	16.200.00
Total sales price	16,200.00

Price	15,300.70	
Accessories	.00	
Doc fee	35.00	
Sales tax	1,265.20	
Service agreement	.00	
Cash price	16,600.90	

***** Payment Schedule *****

Due / Starting		Amount
35	12-30-09	500.00
1	11-30-12	500.00

DMV fees	337.00
Insurance premiums	.00
Total purchase	16,937.90

Amount financed	16,937.90
APR	3.99
Finance charges	1,062.10
Total of payments	18,000.00
Total sales price	18,000.00

Trade-in	.00
Less payoff	.00
Net trade-in	.00
Deferred down	.00
Amount paid now	.00
Total down payment	.00

****

Price	16,835.85
Accessories	.00
Doc fee	35.00
Sales tax	1,391.85
Service agreement	.00
Cash price	18,262.70

***** Payment Schedule *****

Due / Starting		Amount
35	12-30-09	550.00
1	11-30-12	550.00

DMV fees	369.00
Insurance premiums	.00
Total purchase	18,631.70

Amount financed	18,631.70
APR	3.99
Finance charges	1,168.30
Total of payments	19,800.00
Total sales price	19,800.00

Trade-in	.00
Less payoff	.00
Net trade-in	.00
Deferred down	.00
Amount paid now	.00
Total down payment	.00

Price	18,374.68
Accessories	.00
Doc fee	35.00
Sales tax	1,518.80
Service agreement	.00
Cash price	19,928.48
DMV fees	397.00
Insurance premiums	.00
Total purchase	20,325.4
Trade-in	.00
Less payoff	.00
Net trade-in	.00
Deferred down	.00
Amount paid now	.00
Total down payment	.00

***** Payment Schedule *****

Due / Starting		Amount
35	12-30-09	600.00
1	11-30-12	600.00

Amount financed	20,325.48
APR	3.99
Finance charges	1,274.52
Total of payments	21,600.00
Total sales price	21,600.00

****

Price	19,909.82
Accessories	.00
Doc fee	35.00
Sales tax	1,645.45
Service agreement	.00
Cash price	21,590.27
DMV fees	429.00
Insurance premiums	.00
Total purchase	22,019.27
Trade-in	.00
Less payoff	.00
Net trade-in	.00
Deferred down	.00
Amount paid now	.00
Total down payment	.00

***** Payment Schedule *****

Due / Starting		Amount
35	12-30-09	650.00
1	11-30-12	650.00

Amount financed	22,019.27
APR	3.99
Finance charges	1,380.73
Total of payments	23,400.00
Total sales price	23,400.00

Price	21,444.96
Accessories	.00
Doc fee	35.00
Sales tax	1,772.10
Service agreement	.00
Cash price	23,252.06
DMV fees	461.00
Insurance premiums	.00
Total purchase	23,713.06
Trade-in	.00
Less payoff	.00
Net trade-in	.00
Deferred down	.00
Amount paid now	.00
Total down payment	.00

***** Payment Schedule *****

Due / Starting		Amount
35	12-30-09	700.00
1	11-30-12	700.00

Amount financed	23,713.06
APR	3.99
Finance charges	1,486.94
Total of payments	25,200.00
Total sales price	25,200.00

****

Price	22,983.80
Accessories	.00
Doc fee	35.00
Sales tax	1,899.05
Service agreement	.00
Cash price	24,917.85
DMV fees	489.00
Insurance premiums	.00
Total purchase	25,406.85
Trade-in	.00
Less payoff	.00
Net trade-in	.00
Deferred down	.00
Amount paid now	.00
Total down payment	.00

***** Payment Schedule *****

Due / Starting		Amount
35	12-30-09	750.00
1	11-30-12	750.00

Amount financed	25,406.85
APR	3.99
Finance charges	1,593.15
Total of payments	27,000.00
Total sales price	27,000.00

Price	24,518.94
Accessories	.00
Doc fee	35.00
Sales tax	2,025.70
Service agreement	.00
Cash price	26,579.64

DMV fees	521.00
Insurance premiums	.00
Total purchase	27,100.64

Trade-in	.00
Less payoff	.00
Net trade-in	.00
Deferred down	.00
Amount paid now	.00
Total down payment	.00

***** Payment Schedule *****

Due / Starting		Amount
35	12-30-09	800.00
1	11-30-12	800.00

Amount financed	27,100.64
APR	3.99
Finance charges	1,699.36
Total of payments	28,800.00
Total sales price	28,800.00

****

Price	26,054.08
Accessories	.00
Doc fee	35.00
Sales tax	2,152.35
Service agreement	.00
Cash price	28,241.43

DMV fees	553.00
Insurance premiums	.00
Total purchase	28,794.43

Trade-in	.00
Less payoff	.00
Net trade-in	.00
Deferred down	.00
Amount paid now	.00
Total down payment	.00

***** Payment Schedule *****

Due / Starting		Amount
35	12-30-09	850.00
1	11-30-12	850.00

Amount financed	28,794.43
APR	3.99
Finance charges	1,805.57
Total of payments	30,600.00
Total sales price	30,600.00

Price	27,592.92
Accessories	.00
Doc fee	35.00
Sales tax	2,279.30
Service agreement	.00
Cash price	29,907.22

DMV fees	581.00
Insurance premiums	.00
Total purchase	30,488.22

Trade-in	.00
Less payoff	.00
Net trade-in	.00
Deferred down	.00
Amount paid now	.00
Total down payment	.00

***** Payment Schedule *****

Due / Starting		Amount
35	12-30-09	900.00
1	11-30-12	900.00

Amount financed	30,488.22
APR	3.99
Finance charges	1,911.78
Total of payments	32,400.00
Total sales price	32,400.00

****

Price	29,128.06
Accessories	.00
Doc fee	35.00
Sales tax	2,405.95
Service agreement	.00
Cash price	31,569.01

DMV fees	613.00
Insurance premiums	.00
Total purchase	32,182.01

Trade-in	.00
Less payoff	.00
Net trade-in	.00
Deferred down	.00
Amount paid now	.00
Total down payment	.00

***** Payment Schedule *****

Due / Starting		Amount
35	12-30-09	950.00
1	11-30-12	950.00

Amount financed	32,182.01
APR	3.99
Finance charges	2,017.99
Total of payments	34,200.00
Total sales price	34,200.00

Price	30,663.20
Accessories	.00
Doc fee	35.00
Sales tax	2,532.60
Service agreement	.00
Cash price	33,230.80
DMV fees	645.00
Insurance premiums	.00
Total purchase	33,875.00
Trade-in	.00
Less payoff	.00
Net trade-in	.00
Deferred down	.00
Amount paid now	.00
Total down payment	.00

***** Payment Schedule *****

Due / Starting		Amount
35	12-30-09	1,000.00
1	11-30-12	1,000.00

Amount financed	33,875.80
APR	3.99
Finance charges	2,124.20
Total of payments	36,000.00
Total sales price	36,000.00

Saving money on clean, natural gas transportation is the only way for our family to grow up healthy. Making a cleaner America is best for our country. Life is good!

Payment Charts at 4.9% at 48 Months

Price	3,880.82
Accessories	.00
Doc fee	35.00
Sales tax	323.06
Service agreement	.00
Cash price	4,238.88

DMV fees	109.00
Insurance premiums	.00
Total purchase	4,347.88

Trade-in	.00
Less payoff	.00
Net trade-in	.00
Deferred down	.00
Amount paid now	.00
Total down payment	.00

***** Payment Schedule *****

Due / Starting		Amount
47	12-30-09	100.00
1	11-30-13	100.00

Amount financed	4,347.88
APR	4.94
Finance charges	452.12
Total of payments	4,800.00
Total sales price	4,800.00

****

Price	5,852.12
Accessories	.00
Doc fee	35.00
Sales tax	485.69
Service agreement	.00
Cash price	6,372.81

DMV fees	149.00
Insurance premiums	.00
Total purchase	6,521.81

Trade-in	.00
Less payoff	.00
Net trade-in	.00
Deferred down	.00
Amount paid now	.00
Total down payment	.00

***** Payment Schedule *****

Due / Starting		Amount
47	12-30-09	150.00
1	11-30-13	150.00

Amount financed	6,521.81
APR	4.94
Finance charges	678.19
Total of payments	7,200.00
Total sales price	7,200.00

Price	7,823.43
Accessories	.00
Doc fee	35.00
Sales tax	648.32
Service agreement	.00
Cash price	8,506.75
DMV fees	189.00
Insurance premiums	.00
Total purchase	8,695.75
Trade-in	.00
Less payoff	.00
Net trade-in	.00
Deferred down	.00
Amount paid now	.00
Total down payment	.00

***** Payment Schedule *****

Due / Starting		Amount
47	12-30-09	200.00
1	11-30-13	200.00

Amount financed	8,695.75
APR 4.94	
Finance charges	904.25
Total of payments	9,600.00
Total sales price	9,600.00

****

Price	9,798.43
Accessories	.00
Doc fee	35.00
Sales tax	811.26
Service agreement	.00
Cash price	10,644.69
DMV fees	225.00
Insurance premiums	.00
Total purchase	10,869.69
Trade-in	.00
Less payoff	.00
Net trade-in	.00
Deferred down	.00
Amount paid now	.00
Total down payment	.00

***** Payment Schedule *****

Due / Starting		Amount
47	12-30-09	250.00
1	11-30-13	250.00

Amount financed	10,869.69
APR	4.94
Finance charges	1,130.31
Total of payments	12,000.00
Total sales price	12,000.00

Price	11,769.74
Accessories	.00
Doc fee	35.00
Sales tax	973.89
Service agreement	.00
Cash price	12,778.63

DMV fees	265.00
Insurance premiums	.00
Total purchase	13,043.63

Trade-in	.00
Less payoff	.00
Net trade-in	.00
Deferred down	.00
Amount paid now	.00
Total down payment	.00

***** Payment Schedule *****

Due / Starting		Amount
47	12-30-09	300.00
1	11-30-13	300.00

Amount financed	13,043.63
APR	4.94
Finance charges	1,356.37
Total of payments	14,400.00
Total sales price	14,400.00

****

Price	13,741.04
Accessories	.00
Doc fee	35.00
Sales tax	1,136.52
Service agreement	.00
Cash price	14,912.36

DMV fees	305.00
Insurance premiums	.00
Total purchase	15,217.56

Trade-in	.00
Less payoff	.00
Net trade-in	.00
Deferred down	.00
Amount paid now	.00
Total down payment	.00

***** Payment Schedule *****

Due / Starting		Amount
47	12-30-09	350.00
1	11-30-13	350.00

Amount financed	15,217.56
APR	4.94
Finance charges	1,582.44
Total of payments	16,800.00
Total sales price	16,800.00

Price	15,712.35	
Accessories	.00	
Doc fee	35.00	
Sales tax	1,299.16	
Service agreement	.00	
Cash price	17,046.51	

***** Payment Schedule *****

Due / Starting		Amount
47	12-30-09	400.00
1	11-30-13	400.00

DMV fees	345.00
Insurance premiums	.00
Total purchase	17,391.51

Amount financed	17,391.51
APR	4.94
Finance charges	1,808.49
Total of payments	19,200.00
Total sales price	19,200.00

Trade-in	.00
Less payoff	.00
Net trade-in	.00
Deferred down	.00
Amount paid now	.00
Total down payment	.00

Price	17,683.65
Accessories	.00
Doc fee	35.00
Sales tax	1,461.79
Service agreement	.00
Cash price	19,180.44

***** Payment Schedule *****

Due / Starting		Amount
47	12-30-09	450.00
1	11-30-13	450.00

DMV fees	385.00
Insurance premiums	.00
Total purchase	19,565.44

Amount financed	19,565.44
APR	4.94
Finance charges	2,034.56
Total of payments	21,600.00
Total sales price	21,600.00

Trade-in	.00
Less payoff	.00
Net trade-in	.00
Deferred down	.00
Amount paid now	.00
Total down payment	.00

Price	19,654.96	
Accessories	.00	
Doc fee	35.00	
Sales tax	1,624.42	
Service agreement	.00	
Cash price	21,314.38	
DMV fees	425.00	
Insurance premiums	.00	
Total purchase	21,739.38	
Trade-in	.00	
Less payoff	.00	
Net trade-in	.00	
Deferred down	.00	
Amount paid now	.00	
Total down payment	.00	

***** Payment Schedule *****

Due / Starting		Amount
47	12-30-09	500.00
1	11-30-13	500.00

Amount financed	21,739.38
APR	4.94
Finance charges	2,260.62
Total of payments	24,000.00
Total sales price	24,000.00

****

Price	21,626.27	
Accessories	.00	
Doc fee	35.00	
Sales tax	1,787.05	
Service agreement	.00	
Cash price	23,448.32	
DMV fees	465.00	
Insurance premiums	.00	
Total purchase	23,913.32	
Trade-in	.00	
Less payoff	.00	
Net trade-in	.00	
Deferred down	.00	
Amount paid now	.00	
Total down payment	.00	

***** Payment Schedule *****

Due / Starting		Amount
47	12-30-09	550.00
1	11-30-13	550.00

Amount financed	23,913.32
APR	4.94
Finance charges	2,486.68
Total of payments	26,400.00
Total sales price	26,400.00

		***** Payment Schedule *****	
Price	23,601.27		
Accessories	.00		
Doc fee	35.00	Due / Starting	Amount
Sales tax	1,949.99		
Service agreement	.00	47 12-30-09	600.00
Cash price	25,586.26	1 11-30-13	600.00
DMV fees	505.00	Amount financed	26,091.26
Insurance premiums	.00	APR	4.94
Total purchase	26,091.26	Finance charges	2,708.74
		Total of payments	28,000.00
		Total sales price	28,000.00
Trade-in	.00		
Less payoff	.00		
Net trade-in	.00		
Deferred down	.00		
Amount paid now	.00		
Total down payment	.00		

****

		***** Payment Schedule *****	
Price	25,572.57		
Accessories	.00		
Doc fee	35.00	Due / Starting	Amount
Sales tax	2,112.62		
Service agreement	.00	47 12-30-09	650.00
Cash price	27,720.19	1 11-30-13	650.00
DMV fees	541.00	Amount financed	28,261.19
Insurance premiums	.00	APR	4.94
Total purchase	28,261.19	Finance charges	2,938.81
		Total of payments	31,200.00
		Total sales price	31,200.00
Trade-in	.00		
Less payoff	.00		
Net trade-in	.00		
Deferred down	.00		
Amount paid now	.00		
Total down payment	.00		

BUYERS VS. LIARS

		***** Payment Schedule *****	
e	31,486.49		
essories	.00		
fee	35.00	**Due / Starting**	**Amount**
es tax	2,600.52		
vice agreement	.00	47 12-30-09	800.00
h price	34,122.01	1 11-30-13	800.00
V fees	661.00	Amount financed	34,783.01
urance premiums	.00	APR	4.94
al purchase	34,783.01	Finance charges	3,616.99
		Total of payments	38,400.00
		Total sales price	38,400.00
de-in	.00		
s payoff	.00		
trade-in	.00		
erred down	.00		
ount paid now	.00		
al down payment	.00		

****

		***** Payment Schedule *****	
e	33,457.79		
essories	.00		
c fee	35.00	**Due / Starting**	**Amount**
es tax	2,763.16		
vice agreement	.00	47 12-30-09	850.00
h price	36,255.95	1 11-30-13	850.00
V fees	701.00	Amount financed	36,956.95
urance premiums	.00	APR	4.94
al purchase	36,956.95	Finance charges	3,843.05
		Total of payments	40,800.00
		Total sales price	40,800.00
de-in	.00		
s payoff	.00		
trade-in	.00		
erred down	.00		
ount paid now	.00		
al down payment	.00		

Price	27,543.88	***** Payment S	
Accessories	.00		
Doc fee	35.00	Due / Starting	
Sales tax	2,275.26		
Service agreement	.00	47 12-30-09	
Cash price	29,854.14	1 11-30-13	
DMV fees	581.00	Amount financed	
Insurance premiums	.00	APR	
Total purchase	30,435.14	Finance charges	
		Total of payments	
		Total sales price	
Trade-in	.00		
Less payoff	.00		
Net trade-in	.00		
Deferred down	.00		
Amount paid now	.00		
Total down payment	.00		

****

Price	29,515.18	***** Payment	
Accessories	.00		
Doc fee	35.00	Due / Starting	
Sales tax	2,437.89		
Service agreement	.00	47 12-30-09	
Cash price	31,988.07	1 11-30-13	
DMV fees	621.00	Amount financed	
Insurance premiums	.00	APR	
Total purchase	32,609.07	Finance charges	
		Total of payment	
		Total sales price	
Trade-in	.00		
Less payoff	.00		
Net trade-in	.00		
Deferred down	.00		
Amount paid now	.00		
Total down payment	.00		

Price	35,429.10
Accessories	.00
Doc fee	35.00
Sales tax	2,925.79
Service agreement	.00
Cash price	38,389.89
DMV fees	741.00
Insurance premiums	.00
Total purchase	39,130.89
Trade-in	.00
Less payoff	.00
Net trade-in	.00
Deferred down	.00
Amount paid now	.00
Total down payment	.00

***** Payment Schedule *****

Due / Starting		Amount
47	12-30-09	900.00
1	11-30-13	900.00

Amount financed	39,130.89
APR	4.94
Finance charges	4,069.11
Total of payments	43,200.00
Total sales price	43,200.00

****

Price	37,400.41
Accessories	.00
Doc fee	35.00
Sales tax	3,088.42
Service agreement	.00
Cash price	40,523.83
DMV fees	781.00
Insurance premiums	.00
Total purchase	41,304.83
Trade-in	.00
Less payoff	.00
Net trade-in	.00
Deferred down	.00
Amount paid now	.00
Total down payment	

***** Payment Schedule *****

Due / Starting		Amount
47	12-30-09	950.00
1	11-30-13	950.00

Amount financed	41,304.83
APR	4.94
Finance charges	4,295.17
Total of payments	45,600.00
Total sales price	45,600.00

Price	39,375.41
Accessories	.00
Doc fee	35.00
Sales tax	3,251.36
Service agreement	.00
Cash price	42,661.77

DMV fees	817.00
Insurance premiums	.00
Total purchase	43,478.77

Trade-in	.00
Less payoff	.00
Net trade-in	.00
Deferred down	.00
Amount paid now	.00
Total down payment	.00

***** Payment Schedule *****

Due / Starting		Amount
47	12-30-09	1,000.00
1	11-30-13	1,000.00

Amount financed	43,478.77
APR	4.94
Finance charges	4,521.23
Total of payments	48,000.00
Total sales price	48,000.00

All citizens should have the *Buyers vs. Liars* information and buying guide in their homes. It's about the inside knowledge.

Chapter 9

This chapter is a main part of this book because it has the 60 months payment schedule chart. Always go with the 60 months monthly term first to see what your monthly payments are before you look at 72 or 84 months. Make sure that you get the seven years and 100,000 miles with $0 deductible or maximum warranty before going into the finance department. If your interest rates are over 7.95%, it's best to make sure that you have GAP insurance on your vehicle. This is a must-have information-buying guide!

Look at all items on the printout! This is where thousands of dollars will be saved for the consumers of America.

Payment Schedule Charts at 0% for 60 Months

0% financing is usually more like 0.19% so the bank can make a little money. Remember, nothing in life is free!

Price	10,879.52
Accessories	.00
Doc fee	55.00
Dealer smog	29.00
Sales tax	904.48
Service agreement	.00
Cash price	11,868.00

***** Payment Schedule *****

Due / Starting		Amount
59	12-30-09	200.00
1	11-30-14	200.00

DMV fees	132.00
Insurance premiums	.00
Total purchase	12,000.00

Amount financed	12,000.00
APR	0.00
Finance charges	.00
Total of payments	12,000.00
Total sales price	12,000.00

Trade-in	.00
Less payoff	.00
Net trade-in	.00
Deferred down	.00
Amount paid now	.00
Total down payment	.00

****

Price	13,639.79
Accessories	.00
Doc fee	55.00
Dealer smog	29.00
Sales tax	1,132.21
Service agreement	.00
Cash price	14,856.00

***** Payment Schedule *****

Due / Starting		Amount
59	12-30-09	250.00
1	11-30-14	250.00

DMV fees	144.00
Insurance premiums	.00
Total purchase	15,000.00

Amount financed	15,000.00
APR	0.00
Finance charges	.00
Total of payments	15,000.00
Total sales price	15,000.00

Trade-in	.00
Less payoff	.00
Net trade-in	.00
Deferred down	.00
Amount paid now	.00
Total down payment	.00

Price	16,389.91
Accessories	.00
Doc fee	55.00
Dealer smog	29.00
Sale tax	1,359.09
Service agreement	.00
Cash price	17,833.00

DMV fees	167.00
Insurance premiums	.00
Total purchase	18,000.00

Trade-in	.00
Less payoff	.00
Net trade-in	.00
Deferred down	.00
Amount paid now	.00
Total down payment	.00

***** Payment Schedule *****

Due / Starting		Amount
59	12-30-09	300.00
1	11-30-14	300.00

Amount financed	18,000.00
APR	0.00
Finance charges	.00
Total of payments	18,000.00
Total sales price	18,000.00

****

Price	19,150.18
Accessories	.00
Doc fee	55.00
Dealer smog	29.00
Sales tax	1,586.82
Service agreement	.00
Cash price	20,821.00

DMV fees	179.00
Insurance premiums	.00
Total purchase	21,000.00

Trade-in	.00
Less payoff	.00
Net trade-in	.00
Deferred down	.00
Amount paid now	.00
Total down payment	.00

***** Payment Schedule *****

Due / Starting		Amount
59	12-30-09	350.00
1	11-30-14	350.00

Amount financed	21,000.00
APR	0.00
Finance charges	.00
Total of payments	21,000.00
Total sales price	21,000.00

Price	21,904.92
Accessories	.00
Doc fee	55.00
Dealer smog	29.00
Sales tax	1,814.08
Service agreement	.00
Cash price	23,803.00

DMV fees	197.00
Insurance premiums	.00
Total purchase	24,000.00

Trade-in	.00
Less payoff	.00
Net trade-in	.00
Deferred down	.00
Amount paid now	.00
Total down payment	.00

***** Payment Schedule *****

Due / Starting		Amount
59 12-30-09		400.00
1 11-30-14		400.00

Amount financed	24,000.00
APR	0.00
Finance charges	.00
Total of payments	24,000.00
Total sale price	24,000.00

****

Price	24,658.73
Accessories	.00
Doc fee	55.00
Dealer smog	29.00
Sales tax	2,041.27
Service agreement	.00
Cash price	26,784.00

DMV fees	216.00
Insurance premiums	.00
Total purchase	27,000.00

Trade-in	.00
Less payoff	.00
Net trade-in	.00
Deferred down	.00
Amount paid now	.00
Total down payment	.00

***** Payment Schedule *****

Due / Starting		Amount
59 12-30-09		450.00
1 11-30-14		450.00

Amount financed	27,000.00
APR	0.00
Finance charges	.00
Total of payments	27,000.00
Total sales price	27,000.00

Price	27,415.31
Accessories	.00
Doc fee	55.00
Dealer smog	29.00
Sale tax	2,268.69
Service agreement	.00
Cash price	29,768.00
DMV fees	232.00
Insurance premiums	.00
Total purchase	30,000.00
Trade-in	.00
Less payoff	.00
Net trade-in	.00
Deferred down	.00
Amount paid now	.00
Total down payment	.00

***** Payment Schedule *****

Due / Starting		Amount
59	12-30-09	500.00
1	11-30-14	500.00

Amount financed	30,000.00
APR	0.00
Finance charges	.00
Total of payments	30,000.00
Total sales price	30,000.00

****

Price	30,169.10
Accessories	.00
Doc fee	55.00
Dealer smog	29.00
Sales tax	2,495.88
Service agreement	.00
Cash price	32,749.00
DMV fees	251.00
Insurance premiums	.00
Total purchase	33,000.00
Trade-in	.00
Less payoff	.00
Net trade-in	.00
Deferred down	.00
Amount paid now	.00
Total down payment	.00

***** Payment Schedule *****

Due / Starting		Amount
59	12-30-09	550.00
1	11-30-14	550.00

Amount financed	33,000.00
APR	0.00
Finance charges	.00
Total of payments	33,000.00
Total sales price	33,000.00

Price	32,923.85
Accessories	.00
Doc fee	55.00
Dealer smog	29.00
Sales tax	2,723.15
Service agreement	.00
Cash price	35,731.00
DMV fees	269.00
Insurance premiums	.00
Total purchase	36,000.00
Trade-in	.00
Less payoff	.00
Net trade-in	.00
Deferred down	.00
Amount paid now	.00
Total down payment	.00

***** Payment Schedule *****

Due / Starting		Amount
59	12-30-09	600.00
1	11-30-14	600.00

Amount financed	36,000.00
APR	0.00
Finance charges	.00
Total of payments	36,000.00
Total sales price	36,000.00

****

Price	35,678.59
Accessories	.00
Doc fee	55.00
Dealer smog	29.00
Sales tax	2,950.41
Service agreement	.00
Cash price	38,713.00
DMV fees	287.00
Insurance premiums	.00
Total purchase	39,000.00
Trade-in	.00
Less payoff	.00
Net trade-in	.00
Deferred down	.00
Amount paid now	.00
Total down payment	.00

***** Payment Schedule *****

Due / Starting		Amount
59	12-30-09	650.00
1	11-30-14	650.00

Amount financed	39,000.00
APR	0.00
Finance charges	.00
Total of payments	39,000.00
Total sales price	39,000.00

Price	38,433.32
Accessories	.00
Doc fee	55.00
Dealer smog	29.00
Sales tax	3,177.68
Service agreement	.00
Cash price	41,695.00
DMV fees	305.00
Insurance premiums	.00
Total purchase	45,000.00
Trade-in	.00
Less payoff	.00
Net trade-in	.00
Deferred down	.00
Amount paid now	.00
Total down payment	.00

***** Payment Schedule *****

Due / Starting		Amount
59	12-30-09	700.00
1	11-30-14	700.00

Amount financed	45,000.00
APR	0.00
Finance charges	.00
Total of payments	45,000.00
Total sales price	45,000.00

****

Price	41,188.98
Accessories	.00
Doc fee	55.00
Dealer smog	29.00
Sales tax	3,405.02
Service agreement	.00
Cash price	44,678.00
DMV fees	322.00
Insurance premiums	.00
Total purchase	45,000.00
Trade-in	.00
Less payoff	.00
Net trade-in	.00
Deferred down	.00
Amount paid now	.00
Total down payment	.00

***** Payment Schedule *****

Due / Starting		Amount
59	12-30-09	750.00
1	11-30-14	750.00

Amount financed	45,000.00
APR	0.00
Finance charges	.00
Total of payments	45,000.00
Total sales price	45,000.00

Price	43,943.72
Accessories	.00
Doc fee	55.00
Dealer smog	29.00
Sales tax	3,632.28
Service agreement	.00
Cash price	47,660.00
DMV fees	340.00
Insurance premiums	.00
Total purchase	48,000.00
Trade-in	.00
Less payoff	.00
Net trade-in	.00
Deferred down	.00
Amount paid now	.00
Total down payment	.00

***** Payment Schedule *****

Due / Starting		Amount
59	12-30-09	800.00
1	11-30-14	800.00

Amount financed	48,000.00
APR	0.00
Finance charges	.00
Total of payments	48,000.00
Total sales price	48,000.00

****

Price	46,697.53
Accessories	.00
Doc fee	55.00
Dealer smog	29.00
Sales tax	3,859.47
Service agreement	.00
Cash price	50,641.00
DMV fees	359.00
Insurance premiums	.00
Total purchase	51,000.00
Trade-in	.00
Less payoff	.00
Net trade-in	.00
Deferred down	.00
Amount paid now	.00
Total down payment	.00

***** Payment Schedule *****

Due / Starting		Amount
59	12-30-09	850.00
1	11-30-14	850.00

Amount financed	51,000.00
APR	0.00
Finance charges	.00
Total of payments	51,000.00
Total sales price	51,000.00

Price	49,452.26	***** Payment Schedule *****	
Accessories	.00		
Doc fee	55.00	**Due / Starting**	**Amount**
Dealer smog	29.00		
Sales tax	4,086.74		
Service agreement	.00	59 12-30-09	900.00
Cash price	53,623.00	1 11-30-14	900.00
DMV fees	377.00	Amount financed	54,000.00
Insurance premiums	.00	APR	0.00
Total purchase	54,000.00	Finance charges	.00
		Total of payments	54,000.00
		Total sales price	54,000.00
Trade-in	.00		
Less payoff	.00		
Net trade-in	.00		
Deferred down	.00		
Amount paid now	.00		
Total down payment	.00		

****

Price	52,207.92	***** Payment Schedule *****	
Accessories	.00		
Doc fee	55.00	**Due / Starting**	**Amount**
Dealer smog	29.00		
Sales tax	4,314.08		
Service agreement	.00	59 12-30-09	950.00
Cash price	56,606.00	1 11-30-14	950.00
DMV fees	394.00	Amount financed	57,000.00
Insurance premiums	.00	APR	0.00
Total purchase	57,000.00	Finance charges	.00
		Total of payments	57,000.00
		Total sales price	57,000.00
Trade-in	.00		
Less payoff	.00		
Net trade-in	.00		
Deferred down	.00		
Amount paid now	.00		
Total down payment	.00		

Price	54,962.25
Accessories	.00
Doc fee	55.00
Dealer smog	29.00
Sales tax	4,541.35
Service agreement	.00
Cash price	59,588.00
DMV fees	412.00
Insurance premiums	.00
Total purchase	60,000.00
Trade-in	.00
Less payoff	.00
Net trade-in	.00
Deferred down	.00
Amount paid now	.00
Total down payment	.00

***** Payment Schedule *****

Due / Starting		Amount
59	12-30-09	1,000.00
1	11-30-14	1,000.00

Amount financed	60,000.00
APR	0.00
Finance charges	.00
Total of payments	60,000.00
Total sales price	60,000.00

Our future is for the next generation, and we can't overspend out of our budget. This book, *Buyers vs. Liars,* will teach us to go green and to save our land, our animals, our water, our air, and most of all help us save our next generation.

Payment Schedule Charts at 2.9%
for 60 Months

Price	10,075.81
Accessories	.00
Doc fee	55.00
Dealer smog	29.00
Sales tax	838.18
Service agreement	.00
Cash price	10,913.99

***** Payment Schedule *****

Due / Starting		Amount
59	12-30-09	200.00
1	11-30-14	200.00

DMV fees	121.00
Insurance premiums	.00
Total purchase	11,034.99

Amount financed	11,034.99
APR	2.9
Finance charges	965.01
Total of payments	12,000.00
Total sales price	12,000.00

Trade-in	.00
Less payoff	.00
Net trade-in	.00
Deferred down	.00
Amount paid now	.00
Total down payment	.00

****

Price	12,633.90
Accessories	.00
Doc fee	55.00
Dealer smog	29.00
Sales tax	1,049.26
Service agreement	.00
Cash price	13,762.12

***** Payment Schedule *****

Due / Starting		Amount
59	12-30-09	250.00
1	11-30-14	250.00

DMV fees	138.00
Insurance premiums	.00
Total purchase	13,905.12

Amount financed	13,905.12
APR	2.9
Finance charges	1,097.26
Total of payments	15,000.00
Total sales price	15,000.00

Trade-in	.00
Less payoff	.00
Net trade-in	.00
Deferred down	.00
Amount paid now	.00
Total down payment	.00

Price	15,193.90
Accessories	.00
Doc fee	55.00
Dealer smog	29.00
Sales tax	1,260.42
Service agreement	.00
Cash price	16,538.32

***** Payment Schedule *****

Due / Starting		Amount
59	12-30-09	300.00
1	11-30-14	300.00

DMV fees	153.00
Insurance premiums	.00
Total purchase	16,691.32

Amount financed	16,691.32
APR	2.9
Finance charges	1,309.67
Total of payments	18,000.00
Total sales price	18,000.00

Trade-in	.00
Less payoff	.00
Net trade-in	.00
Deferred down	.00
Amount paid now	.00
Total down payment	.00

****

Price	17,752.25
Accessories	.00
Doc fee	55.00
Dealer smog	29.00
Sales tax	1,471.49
Service agreement	.00
Cash price	19,307.74

***** Payment Schedule *****

Due / Starting		Amount
59	12-30-09	350.00
1	11-30-14	350.00

DMV fees	170.00
Insurance premiums	.00
Total purchase	19,477.74

Amount financed	19,477.74
APR	2.9
Finance charges	1,469.10
Total of payments	21,000.00
Total sales price	21,000.00

Trade-in	.00
Less payoff	.00
Net trade-in	.00
Deferred down	.00
Amount paid now	.00
Total down payment	.00

		***** Payment Schedule *****	
Price	20,310.14		
Accessories	.00		
Doc fee	55.00	**Due / Starting**	**Amount**
Dealer smog	29.00		
Sales tax	1,682.51		
Service agreement	.00	59 12-30-09	400.00
Cash price	22,076.65	1 11-30-14	400.00
DMV fees	187.00	Amount financed	22,263.65
Insurance premiums	.00	APR	2.9
Total purchase	22,263.51	Finance charges	1,763.35
		Total of payments	24,000.00
		Total sales price	24,000.00
Trade-in	.00		
Less payoff	.00		
Net trade-in	.00		
Deferred down	.00		
Amount paid now	.00		
Total down payment	.00		

****

		***** Payment Schedule *****	
Price	22,868.24		
Accessories	.00		
Doc fee	55.00	**Due / Starting**	**Amount**
Dealer smog	29.00		
Sales tax	1,893.55		
Service agreement	.00	59 12-30-09	450.00
Cash price	24,845.79	1 11-30-14	450.00
DMV fees	204.00	Amount financed	25,049.79
Insurance premiums	.00	APR	2.9
Total purchase	25,049.79	Finance charges	1,950.21
		Total of payments	27,000.00
		Total sales price	27,000.00
Trade-in	.00		
Less payoff	.00		
Net trade-in	.00		
Deferred down	.00		
Amount paid now	.00		
Total down payment	.00		

Price	25,426.34
Accessories	.00
Doc fee	55.00
Dealer smog	29.00
Sales tax	2,104.60
Service agreement	.00
Cash price	27,614.94

***** Payment Schedule *****

Due / Starting		Amount
59	12-30-09	500.00
1	11-30-14	500.00

DMV fees	221.00
Insurance premiums	.00
Total purchase	27,835.94

Amount financed	27,838.94
APR	2.9
Finance charges	2,164.06
Total of payments	30,000.00
Total sales price	30,000.00

Trade-in	.00
Less payoff	.00
Net trade-in	.00
Deferred down	.00
Amount paid now	.00
Total down payment	.00

****

Price	27,986.35
Accessories	.00
Doc fee	55.00
Dealer smog	29.00
Sales tax	2,315.80
Service agreement	.00
Cash price	30,386.15

***** Payment Schedule *****

Due / Starting		Amount
59	12-30-09	550.00
1	11-30-14	550.00

DMV fees	236.00
Insurance premiums	.00
Total purchase	30,622.15

Amount financed	30,662.15
APR	2.9
Finance charges	2,377.84
Total of payments	33,000.00
Total sales price	33,000.00

Trade-in	.00
Less payoff	.00
Net trade-in	.00
Deferred down	.00
Amount paid now	.00
Total down payment	.00

Price	30,544.66	

***** Payment Schedule *****

Price	30,544.66		Due / Starting		Amount
Accessories	.00				
Doc fee	55.00				
Dealer smog	29.00				
Sales tax	2,526.86				
Service agreement	.00		59	12-30-09	600.00
Cash price	33,155.52		1	11-30-14	600.00
DMV fees	253.00		Amount financed		33,408.52
Insurance premiums	.00		APR		2.9
Total purchase	33,408.52		Finance charges		2,591.47
			Total of payments		36,000.00
			Total sales price		36,000.00
Trade-in	.00				
Less payoff	.00				
Net trade-in	.00				
Deferred down	.00				
Amount paid now	.00				
Total down payment	.00				

****

***** Payment Schedule *****

Price	33,102.49		Due / Starting		Amount
Accessories	.00				
Doc fee	55.00				
Dealer smog	29.00				
Sales tax	2,733.34				
Service agreement	.00		59	12-30-09	650.00
Cash price	35,919.83		1	11-30-14	650.00
DMV fees	270.00		Amount financed		36,189.83
Insurance premiums	.00		APR		2.9
Total purchase	36,189.83		Finance charges		2,810.16
			Total of payments		39,000.00
			Total sales price		39,000.00
Trade-in	.00				
Less payoff	.00				
Net trade-in	.00				
Deferred down	.00				
Amount paid now	.00				
Total down payment	.00				

Price	35,660.60
Accessories	.00
Doc fee	55.00
Dealer smog	29.00
Sales tax	2,949.92
Service agreement	.00
Cash price	38,693.52

***** Payment Schedule *****

Due / Starting		Amount
59	12-30-09	700.00
1	11-30-14	700.00

DMV fees	287.00
Insurance premiums	.00
Total purchase	38,980.52

Amount financed	38,980.52
APR	2.9
Finance charges	3,019.47
Total of payments	42,000.00
Total sales price	42,000.00

Trade-in	.00
Less payoff	.00
Net trade-in	.00
Deferred down	.00
Amount paid now	.00
Total down payment	.00

****

Price	38,218.77
Accessories	.00
Doc fee	55.00
Dealer smog	29.00
Sales tax	3,159.97
Service agreement	.00
Cash price	41,462.74

***** Payment Schedule *****

Due / Starting		Amount
59	12-30-09	750.00
1	11-30-14	750.00

DMV fees	304.00
Insurance premiums	.00
Total purchase	41,776.74

Amount financed	41,776.74
APR	2.9
Finance charges	3,233.26
Total of payments	45,000.00
Total sales price	45,000.00

Trade-in	.00
Less payoff	.00
Net trade-in	.00
Deferred down	.00
Amount paid now	.00
Total down payment	.00

		***** Payment Schedule *****	
Price	40,777.71		
Accessories	.00		
Doc fee	55.00	Due / Starting	Amount
Dealer smog	29.00		
Sales tax	3,371.09		
Service agreement	.00	59 12-30-09	800.00
Cash price	44,232.80	1 11-30-14	800.00
DMV fees	320.00	Amount financed	44,552.80
Insurance premiums	.00	APR	2.9
Total purchase	44,552.80	Finance charges	3,447.20
		Total of payments	48,000.00
		Total sales price	48,000.00
Trade-in	.00		
Less payoff	.00		
Net trade-in	.00		
Deferred down	.00		
Amount paid now	.00		
Total down payment	.00		

****

		***** Payment Schedule *****	
Price	43,336.74		
Accessories	.00		
Doc fee	55.00	Due / Starting	Amount
Dealer smog	29.00		
Sales tax	3,582.21		
Service agreement	.00	59 12-30-09	850.00
Cash price	47,002.95	1 11-30-14	850.00
DMV fees	336.00	Amount financed	47,338.95
Insurance premiums	.00	APR	2.9
Total purchase	47,338.95	Finance charges	3,661.05
		Total of payments	51,000.00
		Total sales price	51,000.00
Trade-in	.00		
Less payoff	.00		
Net trade-in	.00		
Deferred down	.00		
Amount paid now	.00		
Total down payment	.00		

Price	45,894.91
Accessories	.00
Doc fee	55.00
Dealer smog	29.00
Sales tax	3,793.26
Service agreement	.00
Cash price	49,772.17
DMV fees	353.00
Insurance premiums	.00
Total purchase	50,125.17
Trade-in	.00
Less payoff	.00
Net trade-in	.00
Deferred down	.00
Amount paid now	.00
Total down payment	.00

***** Payment Schedule *****

Due / Starting		Amount
59	12-30-09	900.00
1	11-30-14	900.00

Amount financed	50,125.17
APR	2.9
Finance charges	3,874.83
Total of payments	54,000.00
Total sales price	54,000.00

****

Price	48,452.94
Accessories	.00
Doc fee	55.00
Dealer smog	29.00
Sales tax	4,004.29
Service agreement	.00
Cash price	52,541.23
DMV fees	370.00
Insurance premiums	.00
Total purchase	52,911.23
Trade-in	.00
Less payoff	.00
Net trade-in	.00
Deferred down	.00
Amount paid now	.00
Total down payment	.00

***** Payment Schedule *****

Due / Starting		Amount
59	12-30-09	950.00
1	11-30-14	950.00

Amount financed	52,911.23
APR	2.9
Finance charges	4,088.77
Total of payments	57,000.00
Total sales price	57,000.00

Price	51,010.96
Accessories	.00
Doc fee	55.00
Dealer smog	29.00
Sales tax	4,215.33
Service agreement	.00
Cash price	55,310.29
DMV fees	387.00
Insurance premiums	.00
Total purchase	55,697.29
Trade-in	.00
Less payoff	.00
Net trade-in	.00
Deferred down	.00
Amount paid now	.00
Total down payment	.00

***** Payment Schedule *****

Due / Starting		Amount
59	12-30-09	1,000.00
1	11-30-14	1,000.00

Amount financed	55,697.29
APR	2.9
Finance charges	4,302.71
Total of payments	60,000.00
Total sales price	60,000.00

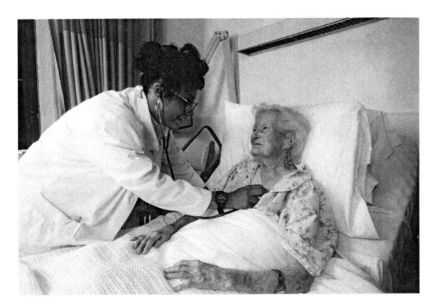

Yes, ma'am, your insurance is covered. Nurse, how's your new vehicle running? The nurse said, "Thanks to the new book that you advised me to read, *Buyers vs. Liars*, we have saved enough money to put down on a new home."

Our world is full of money!
Most of it is in the wrong hands.

Buyers vs. Liars

Saving money is what it's all about.

THE CONSUMER'S BRIDGE TO LIFE!

We can save BILLIONS of dollars by using

Buyers vs. Liars

Payment Schedule Charts at 3.9%
for 60 Months

		***** Payment Schedule *****	
Price	9,823.14		
Accessories	.00		
Doc fee	55.00	Due / Starting	Amount
Dealer smog	29.00		
Sales tax	817.33		
Service agreement	.00	59 12-30-09	200.00
Cash price	10,670.02	1 11-30-14	200.00
DMV fees	119.00	Amount financed	10,789.02
Insurance premiums	.00	APR	3.9
Total purchase	10,789.02	Finance charges	1,120.98
		Total of payments	12,000.00
		Total sales price	12,000.00
Trade-in	.00		
Less payoff	.00		
Net trade-in	.00		
Deferred down	.00		
Amount paid now	.00		
Total down payment	.00		

****

		***** Payment Schedule *****	
Price	12,318.32		
Accessories	.00		
Doc fee	55.00	Due / Starting	Amount
Dealer smog	29.00		
Sales tax	1,023.19		
Service agreement	.00	59 12-30-09	250.00
Cash price	13,425.51	1 11-30-14	250.00
DMV fees	135.00	Amount financed	13,560.51
Insurance premiums	.00	APR	3.9
Total purchase	13,560.51	Finance charges	1,439.49
		Total of payments	15,000.00
		Total sales price	15,000.00
Trade-in	.00		
Less payoff	.00		
Net trade-in	.00		
Deferred down	.00		
Amount paid now	.00		
Total down payment	.00		

Price	14,812.65
Accessories	.00
Doc fee	55.00
Dealer smog	29.00
Sales tax	1,228.97
Service agreement	.00
Cash price	16,125.62
DMV fees	152.00
Insurance premiums	.00
Total purchase	16,277.62
Trade-in	.00
Less payoff	.00
Net trade-in	.00
Deferred down	.00
Amount paid now	.00
Total down payment	.00

***** Payment Schedule *****

Due / Starting		Amount
59	12-30-09	300.00
1	11-30-14	300.00

Amount financed	16,277.62
APR	3.9
Finance charges	1,722.38
Total of payments	18,000.00
Total sales price	18,000.00

****

Price	17,308.98
Accessories	.00
Doc fee	55.00
Dealer smog	29.00
Sales tax	1,434.92
Service agreement	.00
Cash price	18,825.50
DMV fees	167.00
Insurance premiums	.00
Total purchase	18,994.90
Trade-in	.00
Less payoff	.00
Net trade-in	.00
Deferred down	.00
Amount paid now	.00
Total down payment	.00

***** Payment Schedule *****

Due / Starting		Amount
59	12-30-09	350.00
1	11-30-14	350.00

Amount financed	18,994.90
APR	3.9
Finance charges	2,007.10
Total of payments	21,000.00
Total sales price	21,000.00

Price	19,803.20	
Accessories	.00	
Doc fee	55.00	
Dealer smog	29.00	
Sales tax	1,640.69	
Service agreement	.00	
Cash price	21,527.89	
DMV fees	184.00	
Insurance premiums	.00	
Total purchase	21,711.89	
Trade-in	.00	
Less payoff	.00	
Net trade-in	.00	
Deferred down	.00	
Amount paid now	.00	
Total down payment	.00	

***** Payment Schedule *****

Due / Starting		Amount
59	12-30-09	400.00
1	11-30-14	400.00

Amount financed	21,711.89
APR	3.9
Finance charges	2,288.11
Total of payments	24,000.00
Total sales price	24,000.00

****

Price	22,298.70	
Accessories	.00	
Doc fee	55.00	
Dealer smog	29.00	
Sales tax	1,846.57	
Service agreement	.00	
Cash price	24,229.27	
DMV fees	200.00	
Insurance premiums	.00	
Total purchase	24,429.27	
Trade-in	.00	
Less payoff	.00	
Net trade-in	.00	
Deferred down	.00	
Amount paid now	.00	
Total down payment	.00	

***** Payment Schedule *****

Due / Starting		Amount
59	12-30-09	450.00
1	11-30-14	450.00

Amount financed	24,429.27
APR	3.9
Finance charges	2,570.73
Total of payments	27,000.00
Total sales price	27,000.00

Price	24,794.07
Accessories	.00
Doc fee	55.00
Dealer smog	29.00
Sales tax	2,052.44
Service agreement	.00
Cash price	26,930.51
DMV fees	216.00
Insurance premiums	.00
Total purchase	27,146.51
Trade-in	.00
Less payoff	.00
Net trade-in	.00
Deferred down	.00
Amount paid now	.00
Total down payment	.00

***** Payment Schedule *****

Due / Starting		Amount
59	12-30-09	500.00
1	11-30-14	500.00

Amount financed	27,146.51
APR	3.9
Finance charges	2,853.49
Total of payments	30,000.00
Total sales price	30,000.00

****

Price	27,289.41
Accessories	.00
Doc fee	55.00
Dealer smog	29.00
Sales tax	2,258.30
Service agreement	.00
Cash price	29,631.71
DMV fees	232.00
Insurance premiums	.00
Total purchase	29,863.71
Trade-in	.00
Less payoff	.00
Net trade-in	.00
Deferred down	.00
Amount paid now	.00
Total down payment	.00

***** Payment Schedule *****

Due / Starting		Amount
59	12-30-09	550.00
1	11-30-14	550.00

Amount financed	29,863.71
APR	3.9
Finance charges	3,136.29
Total of payments	33,000.00
Total sales price	33,000.00

		***** Payment Schedule *****	
Price	29,784.73		
Accessories	.00		
Doc fee	55.00	Due / Starting	Amount
Dealer smog	29.00		
Sales tax	2,464.17		
Service agreement	.00	59 12-30-09	600.00
Cash price	32,332.90	1 11-30-14	600.00
DMV fees	248.00	Amount financed	32,580.90
Insurance premiums	.00	APR	3.9
Total purchase	32,580.90	Finance charges	3,419.10
		Total of payments	36,000.00
		Total sales price	36,000.00
Trade-in	.00		
Less payoff	.00		
Net trade-in	.00		
Deferred down	.00		
Amount paid now	.00		
Total down payment	.00		

****

		***** Payment Schedule *****	
Price	32,279.16		
Accessories	.00		
Doc fee	55.00	Due / Starting	Amount
Dealer smog	29.00		
Sales tax	2,669.96		
Service agreement	.00	59 12-30-09	650.00
Cash price	35,033.12	1 11-30-14	650.00
DMV fees	265.00	Amount financed	35,298.12
Insurance premiums	.00	APR	3.9
Total purchase	35,298.12	Finance charges	3,701.88
		Total of payments	39,000.00
		Total sales price	39,000.00
Trade-in	.00		
Less payoff	.00		
Net trade-in	.00		
Deferred down	.00		
Amount paid now	.00		
Total down payment	.00		

		***** Payment Schedule *****	
Price	34,774.50		
Accessories	.00		
Doc fee	55.00	Due / Starting	Amount
Dealer smog	29.00		
Sales tax	2,875.82		
Service agreement	.00	59 12-30-09	700.00
Cash price	37,734.32	1 11-30-14	700.00
DMV fees	281.00	Amount financed	38,015.32
Insurance premiums	.00	APR	3.9
Total purchase	38,015.32	Finance charges	3,984.68
		Total of payments	42,000.00
		Total sales price	42,000.00
Trade-in	.00		
Less payoff	.00		
Net trade-in	.00		
Deferred down	.00		
Amount paid now	.00		
Total down payment	.00		

****

		***** Payment Schedule *****	
Price	37,269.83		
Accessories	.00		
Doc fee	55.00	Due / Starting	Amount
Dealer smog	29.00		
Sales tax	3,081.69		
Service agreement	.00	59 12-30-09	750.00
Cash price	40,435.52	1 11-30-14	750.00
DMV fees	297.00	Amount financed	40,732.52
Insurance premiums	.00	APR	3.9
Total purchase	40,732.52	Finance charges	4,267.48
		Total of payments	45,000.00
		Total sales price	45,000.00
Trade-in	.00		
Less payoff	.00		
Net trade-in	.00		
Deferred down	.00		
Amount paid now	.00		
Total down payment	.00		

		***** Payment Schedule *****	
Price	39,765.17		
Accessories	.00		
Doc fee	55.00	**Due / Starting**	**Amount**
Dealer smog	29.00		
Sales tax	3,287.55		
Service agreement	.00	59 12-30-09	800.00
Cash price	43,136.72	1 11-30-14	800.00
DMV fees	313.00	Amount financed	43,449.72
Insurance premiums	.00	APR	3.9
Total purchase	43,449.72	Finance charges	4,550.28
		Total of payments	48,000.00
		Total sales price	48,000.00
Trade-in	.00		
Less payoff	.00		
Net trade-in	.00		
Deferred down	.00		
Amount paid now	.00		
Total down payment	.00		

****

		***** Payment Schedule *****	
Price	42,259.68		
Accessories	.00		
Doc fee	55.00	**Due / Starting**	**Amount**
Dealer smog	29.00		
Sales tax	3,493.35		
Service agreement	.00	59 12-30-09	850.00
Cash price	45,837.03	1 11-30-14	850.00
DMV fees	330.00	Amount financed	46,167.03
Insurance premiums	.00	APR	3.9
Total purchase	46,167.03	Finance charges	4,832.97
		Total of payments	51,000.00
		Total sales price	51,000.00
Trade-in	.00		
Less payoff	.00		
Net trade-in	.00		
Deferred down	.00		
Amount paid now	.00		
Total down payment	.00		

		***** Payment Schedule *****	
Price	44,754.92		
Accessories	.00		
Doc fee	55.00	Due / Starting	Amount
Dealer smog	29.00		
Sales tax	3,699.21		
Service agreement	.00	59 12-30-09	900.00
Cash price	48,538.13	1 11-30-14	900.00
DMV fees	346.00	Amount financed	48,884.13
Insurance premiums	.00	APR	3.9
Total purchase	48,884.13	Finance charges	5,115.87
		Total of payments	54,000.00
		Total sales price	54,000.00
Trade-in	.00		
Less payoff	.00		
Net trade-in	.00		
Deferred down	.00		
Amount paid now	.00		
Total down payment	.00		

****

		***** Payment Schedule *****	
Price	47,250.26		
Accessories	.00		
Doc fee	55.00	Due / Starting	Amount
Dealer smog	29.00		
Sales tax	3,905.07		
Service agreement	.00	59 12-30-09	950.00
Cash price	51,239.33	1 11-30-14	950.00
DMV fees	362.00	Amount financed	51,601.33
Insurance premiums	.00	APR	3.9
Total purchase	51,601.33	Finance charges	5,398.67
		Total of payments	57,000.00
		Total sales price	57,000.00
Trade-in	.00		
Less payoff	.00		
Net trade-in	.00		
Deferred down	.00		
Amount paid now	.00		
Total down payment	.00		

Price	49,745.60		
Accessories	.00		
Doc fee	55.00		
Dealer smog	29.00		
Sales tax	4,110.94		
Service agreement	.00		
Cash price	53,940.54		

***** Payment Schedule *****

Due / Starting		Amount
59	12-30-09	1,000.00
1	11-30-14	1,000.00

DMV fees	378.00
Insurance premiums	.00
Total purchase	54,318.54

Amount financed	54,318.54
APR	3.9
Finance charges	5,681.46
Total of payments	60,000.00
Total sales price	60,000.00

Trade-in	.00
Less payoff	.00
Net trade-in	.00
Deferred down	.00
Amount paid now	.00
Total down payment	.00

Saving money for my child's future is very important. After using *Buyers vs. Liars'* information guide, we saved extra money with very low monthly payments.

Payment Schedule Charts at 5.9%
for 60 Months

Price	9,633.65
Accessories	.00
Doc fee	55.00
Dealer smog	.00
Sales tax	799.31
Service agreement	.00
Cash price	10,487.96
DMV fees	117.00
Insurance premiums	.00
Total purchase	10,604.96

Trade-in	.00
Less payoff	.00
Net trade-in	.00
Deferred down	.00
Amount paid now	.00
Total down payment	.00

***** Payment Schedule *****

Due / Starting		Amount
59	12-30-09	200.00
1	11-30-14	200.00

Amount financed	10,604.96
APR	5.9
Finance charges	1,395.04
Total of payments	12,000.00
Total sales price	12,000.00

****

Price	12,066.61
Accessories	.00
Doc fee	55.00
Dealer smog	.00
Sales tax	1,000.03
Service agreement	.00
Cash price	13,121.64
DMV fees	134.00
Insurance premiums	.00
Total purchase	13,255.64

Trade-in	.00
Less payoff	.00
Net trade-in	.00
Deferred down	.00
Amount paid now	.00
Total down payment	.00

***** Payment Schedule *****

Due / Starting		Amount
59	12-30-09	250.00
1	11-30-14	250.00

Amount financed	13,255.64
APR	5.9
Finance charges	1,744.35
Total of payments	15,000.00
Total sales price	15,000.00

Price	14,501.16	
Accessories	.00	
Doc fee	55.00	
Dealer smog	.00	
Sales tax	1,200.88	
Service agreement	.00	
Cash price	15,752.51	

***** Payment Schedule *****

Due / Starting		Amount
59	12-30-09	300.00
1	11-30-14	300.00

DMV fees	149.00
Insurance premiums	.00
Total purchase	15,906.04

Amount financed	15,906.04
APR	5.9
Finance charges	2,093.96
Total of payments	18,000.00
Total sales price	18,000.00

Trade-in	.00
Less payoff	.00
Net trade-in	.00
Deferred down	.00
Amount paid now	.00
Total down payment	.00

****

Price	16,935.02
Accessories	.00
Doc fee	55.00
Dealer smog	.00
Sales tax	1,401.67
Service agreement	.00
Cash price	18,391.69

***** Payment Schedule *****

Due / Starting		Amount
59	12-30-09	350.00
1	11-30-14	350.00

DMV fees	165.00
Insurance premiums	.00
Total purchase	18,556.69

Amount financed	18,556.69
APR	5.9
Finance charges	2,443.30
Total of payments	21,000.00
Total sales price	21,000.00

Trade-in	.00
Less payoff	.00
Net trade-in	.00
Deferred down	.00
Amount paid now	.00
Total down payment	.00

		***** Payment Schedule *****	
Price	19,314.90		
Accessories	.00		
Doc fee	55.00	Due / Starting	Amount
Dealer smog	.00		
Sales tax	1,598.01		
Service agreement	.00	59 12-30-09	400.00
Cash price	21,967.91	1 11-30-14	400.00
DMV fees	180.00	Amount financed	21,147.91
Insurance premiums	.00	APR	5.9
Total purchase	21,147.91	Finance charges	2,852.09
		Total of payments	24,000.00
		Total sales price	24,000.00
Trade-in	.00		
Less payoff	.00		
Net trade-in	.00		
Deferred down	.00		
Amount paid now	.00		
Total down payment	.00		

****

		***** Payment Schedule *****	
Price	21,803.43		
Accessories	.00		
Doc fee	55.00	Due / Starting	Amount
Dealer smog	.00		
Sales tax	1,803.32		
Service agreement	.00	59 12-30-09	450.00
Cash price	23,661.75	1 11-30-14	450.00
DMV fees	196.00	Amount financed	23,857.75
Insurance premiums	.00	APR	5.9
Total purchase	23,857.75	Finance charges	3,142.25
		Total of payments	27,000.00
		Total sales price	27,000.00
Trade-in	.00		
Less payoff	.00		
Net trade-in	.00		
Deferred down	.00		
Amount paid now	.00		
Total down payment	.00		

Price	24,237.21
Accessories	.00
Doc fee	55.00
Dealer smog	.00
Sales tax	2,004.10
Service agreement	.00
Cash price	26,296.31
DMV fees	212.00
Insurance premiums	.00
Total purchase	26,508.31
Trade-in	.00
Less payoff	.00
Net trade-in	.00
Deferred down	.00
Amount paid now	.00
Total down payment	.00

***** Payment Schedule *****

Due / Starting		Amount
59	12-30-09	500.00
1	11-30-14	500.00

Amount financed	26,508.31
APR	5.9
Finance charges	3,491.69
Total of payments	30,000.00
Total sales price	30,000.00

****

Price	26,670.22
Accessories	.00
Doc fee	55.00
Dealer smog	.00
Sales tax	2,204.83
Service agreement	.00
Cash price	28,930.05
DMV fees	229.00
Insurance premiums	.00
Total purchase	29,159.05
Trade-in	.00
Less payoff	.00
Net trade-in	.00
Deferred down	.00
Amount paid now	.00
Total down payment	.00

***** Payment Schedule *****

Due / Starting		Amount
59	12-30-09	550.00
1	11-30-14	550.00

Amount financed	29,159.05
APR	5.9
Finance charges	3,840.95
Total of payments	33,000.00
Total sales price	33,000.00

		***** Payment Schedule *****	
Price	29,104.76		
Accessories	.00		
Doc fee	55.00	Due / Starting	Amount
Dealer smog	.00		
Sales tax	2,405.68		
Service agreement	.00	59 12-30-09	600.00
Cash price	31,565.44	1 11-30-14	600.00
DMV fees	244.00	Amount financed	31,809.44
Insurance premiums	.00	APR	5.9
Total purchase	31,809.44	Finance charges	4,190.56
		Total of payments	36,000.00
		Total sales price	36,000.00
Trade-in	.00		
Less payoff	.00		
Net trade-in	.00		
Deferred down	.00		
Amount paid now	.00		
Total down payment	.00		

****

		***** Payment Schedule *****	
Price	31,538.55		
Accessories	.00		
Doc fee	55.00	Due / Starting	Amount
Dealer smog	.00		
Sales tax	2,606.46		
Service agreement	.00	59 12-30-09	650.00
Cash price	34,200.01	1 11-30-14	650.00
DMV fees	260.00	Amount financed	34,460.01
Insurance premiums	.00	APR	5.9
Total purchase	34,460.01	Finance charges	4,539.99
		Total of payments	39,000.00
		Total sales price	39,000.00
Trade-in	.00		
Less payoff	.00		
Net trade-in	.00		
Deferred down	.00		
Amount paid now	.00		
Total down payment	.00		

Price	33,973.25
Accessories	.00
Doc fee	55.00
Dealer smog	.00
Sales tax	2,807.33
Service agreement	.00
Cash price	36,835.58

***** Payment Schedule *****

Due / Starting		Amount
59	12-30-09	700.00
1	11-30-14	700.00

DMV fees	275.00
Insurance premiums	.00
Total purchase	37,110.58

Amount financed	37,110.58
APR	5.9
Finance charges	4,889.42
Total of payments	42,000.00
Total sales price	42,000.00

Trade-in	.00
Less payoff	.00
Net trade-in	.00
Deferred down	.00
Amount paid now	.00
Total down payment	.00

****

Price	36,407.03
Accessories	.00
Doc fee	55.00
Dealer smog	.00
Sales tax	3,008.11
Service agreement	.00
Cash price	39,470.14

***** Payment Schedule *****

Due / Starting		Amount
59	12-30-09	750.00
1	11-30-14	750.00

DMV fees	291.00
Insurance premiums	.00
Total purchase	39,761.14

Amount financed	39,761.14
APR	5.9
Finance charges	5,238.86
Total of payments	45,000.00
Total sales price	45,000.00

Trade-in	.00
Less payoff	.00
Net trade-in	.00
Deferred down	.00
Amount paid now	.00
Total down payment	.00

			***** Payment Schedule *****	
Price	38,840.91			
Accessories	.00			
Doc fee	55.00		Due / Starting	Amount
Dealer smog	.00			
Sales tax	3,208.91			
Service agreement	.00		59 12-30-09	800.00
Cash price	42,104.82		1 11-30-14	800.00
DMV fees	307.00		Amount financed	42,411.82
Insurance premiums	.00		APR	5.9
Total purchase	42,411.82		Finance charges	5,588.18
			Total of payments	48,000.00
			Total sales price	48,000.00
Trade-in	.00			
Less payoff	.00			
Net trade-in	.00			
Deferred down	.00			
Amount paid now	.00			
Total down payment	.00			

****

			***** Payment Schedule *****	
Price	41,274.67			
Accessories	.00			
Doc fee	55.00		Due / Starting	Amount
Dealer smog	.00			
Sales tax	3,409.67			
Service agreement	.00		59 12-30-09	850.00
Cash price	44,739.36		1 11-30-14	850.00
DMV fees	323.00		Amount financed	45,062.36
Insurance premiums	.00		APR	5.9
Total purchase	45,062.36		Finance charges	5,937.64
			Total of payments	51,000.00
			Total sales price	51,000.00
Trade-in	.00			
Less payoff	.00			
Net trade-in	.00			
Deferred down	.00			
Amount paid now	.00			
Total down payment	.00			

Price	43,708.37
Accessories	.00
Doc fee	55.00
Dealer smog	.00
Sales tax	3,610.47
Service agreement	.00
Cash price	47,373.84
DMV fees	339.00
Insurance premiums	.00
Total purchase	47,712.84
Trade-in	.00
Less payoff	.00
Net trade-in	.00
Deferred down	.00
Amount paid now	.00
Total down payment	.00

***** Payment Schedule *****

Due / Starting		Amount
59	12-30-09	900.00
1	11-30-14	900.00

Amount financed	47,712.84
APR	5.9
Finance charges	6,287.16
Total of payments	54,000.00
Total sales price	54,000.00

****

Price	46,142.43
Accessories	.00
Doc fee	55.00
Dealer smog	.00
Sales tax	3,811.28
Service agreement	.00
Cash price	50,008.71
DMV fees	355.00
Insurance premiums	
Total purchase	50,363.71
Trade-in	.00
Less payoff	.00
Net trade-in	.00
Deferred down	.00
Amount paid now	.00
Total down payment	.00

***** Payment Schedule *****

Due / Starting		Amount
59	12-30-09	950.00
1	11-30-14	950.00

Amount financed	50,363.71
APR	5.9
Finance charges	6,636.29
Total of payments	57,000.00
Total sales price	57,000.00

		***** Payment Schedule *****	
Price	48,576.85		
Accessories	.00		
Doc fee	55.00	Due / Starting	Amount
Dealer smog	.00		
Sales tax	4,012.12		
Service agreement	.00	59 12-30-09	1,000.00
Cash price	52,643.97	1 11-30-14	1,000.00
DMV fees	370.00	Amount financed	53,013.97
Insurance premiums	.00	APR	5.9
Total purchase	53,013.97	Finance charges	6,986.03
		Total of payments	60,000.00
		Total sales price	60,000.00
Trade-in	.00		
Less payoff	.00		
Net trade-in	.00		
Deferred down	.00		
Amount paid now	.00		
Total down payment	.00		

****

From the White House to Wall Street, we the people need help in building our economy stronger and better than before. Every American must save daily.

Good Credit

The buyer rates are 7.9%, 9%, 11%, and 13%.

When customers have good credit, they should not overextend themselves because of other crises that just might occur. If the dealership gives a customer a high interest rate and she feels that she can get a better rate, she should ask the dealer to send her contract out for an approval from the bank, or she can shop around for a better percentage rate at another dealership. The banks have a buyer rate for the dealers and one for the buying customer as well. Example: The consumer pays an 11.95% rate, but the dealer's buy rate is 8.95%. The dealer just made extra money from the consumer and they don't even know it! The dealership hates for a customer to bolt out of the finance department. Pick the vehicle up when the bank has approved the rate. Demand to see the bank's buy rate approval before signing the contract.

Having good credit at a young age has made all of the difference in my life, thanks to *Buyers vs. Liars*. This book is very important to me. I have learned how to save extra money at an early age in financing my new vehicle. This is a great book!

Payment Schedule Charts at 7.9%
for 60 Months

Price	4,417.05
Accessories	.00
Doc fee	35.00
Sales tax	367.29
Service agreement	.00
Cash price	4,819.34

***** Payment Schedule *****

Due / Starting		Amount
59	12-30-09	100.00
1	11-30-14	100.00

DMV fees	121.00
Insurance premiums	.00
Total purchase	4,940.34

Amount financed	4,940.34
APR	7.9
Finance charges	1,059.66
Total of payments	6,000.00
Total sales price	6,000.00

Trade-in	.00
Less payoff	.00
Net trade-in	.00
Deferred down	.00
Amount paid now	.00
Total down payment	

****

Price	6,685.31
Accessories	.00
Doc fee	35.00
Sales tax	552.20
Service agreement	.00
Cash price	7,245.51

***** Payment Schedule *****

Due / Starting		Amount
59	12-30-09	150.00
1	11-30-14	150.00

DMV fees	165.00
Insurance premiums	.00
Total purchase	7,410.51

Amount financed	7,410.51
APR	7.9
Finance charges	1,589.49
Total of payments	9,000.00
Total sales price	9,000.00

Trade-in	.00
Less payoff	.00
Net trade-in	.00
Deferred down	.00
Amount paid now	.00
Total down payment	

Price	8,899.58
Accessories	.00
Doc fee	35.00
Sales tax	737.10
Service agreement	.00
Cash price	9,671.68
DMV fees	113.00
Insurance premiums	.00
Total purchase	9,784.68
Trade-in	.00
Less payoff	.00
Net trade-in	.00
Deferred down	.00
Amount paid now	.00
Total down payment	

***** Payment Schedule *****

Due / Starting		Amount
59	12-30-09	200.00
1	11-30-14	200.00

Amount financed	9,784.68
APR	7.9
Finance charges	2,215.32
Total of payments	12,000.00
Total sales price	12,000.00

****

Price	11,140.85
Accessories	.00
Doc fee	35.00
Sales tax	922.00
Service agreement	.00
Cash price	12,097.85
DMV fees	127.00
Insurance premiums	.00
Total purchase	12,224.85
Trade-in	.00
Less payoff	.00
Net trade-in	.00
Deferred down	.00
Amount paid now	.00
Total down payment	.00

***** Payment Schedule *****

Due / Starting		Amount
59	12-30-09	250.00
1	11-30-14	250.00

Amount financed	12,224.85
APR	7.9
Finance charges	2,775.15
Total of payments	15,000.00
Total sales price	15,000.00

Price	13,382.12
Accessories	.00
Doc fee	35.00
Sales tax	1,106.91
Service agreement	.00
Cash price	14,524.03

***** Payment Schedule *****

Due / Starting		Amount
59	12-30-09	300.00
1	11-30-14	300.00

DMV fees	143.00
Insurance premiums	.00
Total purchase	14,667.03

Amount financed	14,667.03
APR	7.9
Finance charges	3,332.97
Total of payments	18,000.00
Total sales price	18,000.00

Trade-in	.00
Less payoff	.00
Net trade-in	.00
Deferred down	.00
Amount paid now	.00
Total down payment	.00

****

Price	15,619.69
Accessories	.00
Doc fee	35.00
Sales tax	1,291.51
Service agreement	.00
Cash price	16,946.20

***** Payment Schedule *****

Due / Starting		Amount
59	12-30-09	350.00
1	11-30-14	350.00

DMV fees	157.00
Insurance premiums	.00
Total purchase	17,103.20

Amount financed	17,103.20
APR	7.9
Finance charges	3,896.80
Total of payments	21,000.00
Total sales price	21,000.00

Trade-in	.00
Less payoff	.00
Net trade-in	.00
Deferred down	.00
Amount paid now	.00
Total down payment	.00

Price	17,860.96
Accessories	.00
Doc fee	35.00
Sales tax	1,476.41
Service agreement	.00
Cash price	19,372.37

DMV fees	171.00
Insurance premiums	.00
Total purchase	19,543.37

Trade-in	.00
Less payoff	.00
Net trade-in	.00
Deferred down	.00
Amount paid now	.00
Total down payment	.00

***** Payment Schedule *****

Due / Starting		Amount
59	12-30-09	400.00
1	11-30-14	400.00

Amount financed	19,543.37
APR	7.9
Finance charges	4,456.63
Total of payments	24,000.00
Total sales price	24,000.00

****

Price	20,102.22
Accessories	.00
Doc fee	35.00
Sales tax	1,661.32
Service agreement	.00
Cash price	21,798.54

DMV fees	187.00
Insurance premiums	.00
Total purchase	22,985.54

Trade-in	.00
Less payoff	.00
Net trade-in	.00
Deferred down	.00
Amount paid now	.00
Total down payment	.00

***** Payment Schedule *****

Due / Starting		Amount
59	12-30-09	450.00
1	11-30-14	450.00

Amount financed	22,985.54
APR	7.9
Finance charges	5,014.46
Total of payments	27,000.00
Total sales price	27,000.00

		***** Payment Schedule *****	
Price	22,343.49		
Accessories	.00		
Doc fee	35.00	Due / Starting	Amount
Sales tax	1,846.22		
Service agreement	.00	59 12-30-09	500.00
Cash price	24,224.71	1 11-30-14	500.00
DMV fees	216.00	Amount financed	24,440.71
Insurance premiums	.00	APR	7.9
Total purchase	24,440.71	Finance charges	5,559.29
		Total of payments	30,000.00
		Total sales price	30,000.00
Trade-in	.00		
Less payoff	.00		
Net trade-in	.00		
Deferred down	.00		
Amount paid now	.00		
Total down payment	.00		

****

		***** Payment Schedule *****	
Price	24,584.76		
Accessories	.00		
Doc fee	35.00	Due / Starting	Amount
Sales tax	2,031.13		
Service agreement	.00	59 12-30-09	550.00
Cash price	26,650.89	1 11-30-14	550.00
DMV fees	232.00	Amount financed	26,882.89
Insurance premiums	.00	APR	7.9
Total purchase	26,882.89	Finance charges	6,117.11
		Total of payments	33,000.00
		Total sales price	33,000.00
Trade-in	.00		
Less payoff	.00		
Net trade-in	.00		
Deferred down	.00		
Amount paid now	.00		
Total down payment	.00		

		***** Payment Schedule *****	
Price	26,822.33		
Accessories	.00		
Doc fee	35.00	Due / Starting	Amount
Sales tax	2,215.72		
Service agreement	.00	59 12-30-09	600.00
Cash price	29,073.05	1 11-30-14	600.00
DMV fees	245.00	Amount financed	29,318.05
Insurance premiums	.00	APR	7.9
Total purchase	29,318.05	Finance charges	6,681.95
		Total of payments	36,000.00
		Total sales price	36,000.00
Trade-in	.00		
Less payoff	.00		
Net trade-in	.00		
Deferred down	.00		
Amount paid now	.00		
Total down payment	.00		

****

		***** Payment Schedule *****	
Price	29,063.60		
Accessories	.00		
Doc fee	35.00	Due / Starting	Amount
Sales tax	2,400.63		
Service agreement	.00	59 12-30-09	650.00
Cash price	31,499.23	1 11-30-14	650.00
DMV fees	261.00	Amount financed	31,760.23
Insurance premiums	.00	APR	7.9
Total purchase	31,760.23	Finance charges	7,239.77
		Total of payments	39,000.00
		Total sales price	39,000.00
Trade-in	.00		
Less payoff	.00		
Net trade-in	.00		
Deferred down	.00		
Amount paid now	.00		
Total down payment	.00		

Price	31,514.62
Accessories	.00
Doc fee	35.00
Sales tax	2,602.84
Service agreement	.00
Cash price	34,152.46
DMV fees	274.00
Insurance premiums	.00
Total purchase	34,426.46
Trade-in	.00
Less payoff	.00
Net trade-in	.00
Deferred down	.00
Amount paid now	.00
Total down payment	

***** Payment Schedule *****

Due / Starting		Amount
59	12-30-09	700.00
1	11-30-14	700.00

Amount financed	34,426.46
APR	7.9
Finance charges	7,573.54
Total of payments	42,000.00
Total sales price	42,000.00

****

Price	33,777.56
Accessories	.00
Doc fee	35.00
Sales tax	2,789.53
Service agreement	.00
Cash price	36,602.09
DMV fees	290.00
Insurance premiums	.00
Total purchase	36,892.09
Trade-in	.00
Less payoff	.00
Net trade-in	.00
Deferred down	.00
Amount paid now	.00
Total down payment	.00

***** Payment Schedule *****

Due / Starting		Amount
59	12-30-09	750.00
1	11-30-14	750.00

Amount financed	36,892.09
APR	7.9
Finance charges	8,107.91
Total of payments	45,000.00
Total sales price	45,000.00

Price	36,038.68
Accessories	.00
Doc fee	35.00
Sales tax	2,976.07
Service agreement	.00
Cash price	39,049.75
DMV fees	304.00
Insurance premiums	.00
Total purchase	39,353.75
Trade-in	.00
Less payoff	.00
Net trade-in	.00
Deferred down	.00
Amount paid now	.00
Total down payment	.00

***** Payment Schedule *****

Due / Starting		Amount
59	12-30-09	800.00
1	11-30-14	800.00

Amount financed	39,353.75
APR	7.9
Finance charges	8,646.25
Total of payments	48,000.00
Total sales price	48,000.00

****

Price	38,301.62
Accessories	.00
Doc fee	35.00
Sales tax	3,162.77
Service agreement	.00
Cash price	41,499.39
DMV fees	318.00
Insurance premiums	.00
Total purchase	41,817.39
Trade-in	.00
Less payoff	.00
Net trade-in	.00
Deferred down	.00
Amount paid now	.00
Total down payment	.00

***** Payment Schedule *****

Due / Starting		Amount
59	12-30-09	850.00
1	11-30-14	850.00

Amount financed	41,817.39
APR	7.9
Finance charges	9,182.61
Total of payments	51,000.00
Total sales price	51,000.00

Price	40,564.56
Accessories	.00
Doc fee	35.00
Sales tax	3,349.46
Service agreement	.00
Cash price	43,948.02
DMV fees	348.00
Insurance premiums	.00
Total purchase	44,297.02
Trade-in	.00
Less payoff	.00
Net trade-in	.00
Deferred down	.00
Amount paid now	.00
Total down payment	

***** Payment Schedule *****

Due / Starting		Amount
59	12-30-09	900.00
1	11-30-14	900.00

Amount financed	44,297.02
APR	7.9
Finance charges	9,702.98
Total of payments	54,000.00
Total sales price	54,000.00

****

Price	42,825.66
Accessories	.00
Doc fee	35.00
Sales tax	3,536.00
Service agreement	.00
Cash price	46,396.66
DMV fees	364.00
Insurance premiums	.00
Total purchase	46,760.66
Trade-in	.00
Less payoff	.00
Net trade-in	.00
Deferred down	.00
Amount paid now	.00
Total down payment	.00

***** Payment Schedule *****

Due / Starting		Amount
59	12-30-09	950.00
1	11-30-14	950.00

Amount financed	46,760.66
APR	7.9
Finance charges	10,239.34
Total of payments	57,000.00
Total sales price	57,000.00

Price	45,088.68
Accessories	.00
Doc fee	35.00
Sales tax	3,722.70
Service agreement	.00
Cash price	48,846.38
DMV fees	380.00
Insurance premiums	.00
Total purchase	49,226.38
Trade-in	.00
Less payoff	.00
Net trade-in	.00
Deferred down	.00
Amount paid now	.00
Total down payment	

***** Payment Schedule *****

Due / Starting		Amount
59	12-30-09	1,000.00
1	11-30-14	1,000.00

Amount financed	49,226.38
APR	7.9
Finance charges	10,773.62
Total of payments	60,000.00
Total sales price	60,000.00

Saving money is what we are all about. We all used *Buyers vs. Liars'* information guide, and it has saved us a lot of money on our new drop-top convertible ride. You should do the same!

Thanks, *Buyers vs. Liars!* The book made our life a little easier, and now we are living our lives together and saving money as well! Love on a chopper is cool.

Payment Schedule Charts at 9.9% for 60 Months

Price	8,525.83
Accessories	.00
Doc fee	55.00
Dealer smog	.00
Sales tax	707.91
Service agreement	.00
Cash price	9,288.74

DMV fees	108.00
Insurance premiums	.00
Total purchase	9,396.74

Trade-in	.00
Less payoff	.00
Net trade-in	.00
Deferred down	.00
Amount paid now	.00
Total down payment	.00

***** Payment Schedule *****

Due / Starting		Amount
59	12-30-09	200.00
1	11-30-14	200.00

Amount financed	9,396.74
APR	9.9
Finance charges	2,603.26
Total of payments	12,000.00
Total sales price	12,000.00

****

Price	10,682.11
Accessories	.00
Doc fee	55.00
Dealer smog	.00
Sales tax	885.81
Service agreement	.00
Cash price	11,622.92

DMV fees	125.00
Insurance premiums	.00
Total purchase	11,747.92

Trade-in	.00
Less payoff	.00
Net trade-in	.00
Deferred down	.00
Amount paid now	.00
Total down payment	.00

***** Payment Schedule *****

Due / Starting		Amount
59	12-30-09	250.00
1	11-30-14	250.00

Amount financed	11,747.92
APR	9.9
Finance charges	3,252.08
Total of payments	15,000.00
Total sales price	15,000.00

Price	12,840.04
Accessories	.00
Doc fee	55.00
Dealer smog	.00
Sales tax	1,063.84
Service agreement	.00
Cash price	13,958.88

DMV fees	138.00
Insurance premiums	.00
Total purchase	14,096.88

Trade-in	.00
Less payoff	.00
Net trade-in	.00
Deferred down	.00
Amount paid now	.00
Total down payment	.00

***** Payment Schedule *****

Due / Starting		Amount
59	12-30-09	300.00
1	11-30-14	300.00

Amount financed	14,096.88
APR	9.9
Finance charges	3,903.12
Total of payments	18,000.00
Total sales price	18,000.00

****

Price	14,997.12
Accessories	.00
Doc fee	55.00
Dealer smog	.00
Sales tax	1,241.79
Service agreement	.00
Cash price	16,293.91

DMV fees	152.00
Insurance premiums	.00
Total purchase	16,449.91

Trade-in	.00
Less payoff	.00
Net trade-in	.00
Deferred down	.00
Amount paid now	.00
Total down payment	.00

***** Payment Schedule *****

Due / Starting		Amount
59	12-30-09	350.00
1	11-30-14	350.00

Amount financed	16,449.91
APR	9.9
Finance charges	4,554.09
Total of payments	21,000.00
Total sales price	21,000.00

Price	17,079.20	***** **Payment Schedule** *****		
Accessories	.00			
Doc fee	55.00	**Due / Starting**		**Amount**
Dealer smog	.00			
Sales tax	1,413.57			
Service agreement	.00	59	12-30-09	400.00
Cash price	18,547.77	1	11-30-14	400.00
DMV fees	166.00	**Amount financed**		18,713.77
Insurance premiums	.00	**APR**		9.9
Total purchase	18,713.77	**Finance charges**		5,286.23
		Total of payments		24,000.00
		Total sales price		24,000.00
Trade-in	.00			
Less payoff	.00			
Net trade-in	.00			
Deferred down	.00			
Amount paid now	.00			
Total down payment	.00			

****

Price	19,311.28	***** **Payment Schedule** *****		
Accessories	.00			
Doc fee	55.00	**Due / Starting**		**Amount**
Dealer smog	.00			
Sales tax	1,597.71			
Service agreement	.00	59	12-30-09	450.00
Cash price	20,963.99	1	11-30-14	450.00
DMV fees	180.00	**Amount financed**		21,143.99
Insurance premiums	.00	**APR**		9.9
Total purchase	21,143.99	**Finance charges**		5,856.01
		Total of payments		27,000.00
		Total sales price		27,000.00
Trade-in	.00			
Less payoff	.00			
Net trade-in	.00			
Deferred down	.00			
Amount paid now	.00			
Total down payment	.00			

Price	21,467.51
Accessories	.00
Doc fee	55.00
Dealer smog	.00
Sales tax	1,775.60
Service agreement	.00
Cash price	23,298.11

DMV fees	195.00
Insurance premiums	.00
Total purchase	23,493.11

Trade-in	.00
Less payoff	.00
Net trade-in	.00
Deferred down	.00
Amount paid now	.00
Total down payment	.00

***** Payment Schedule *****

Due / Starting		Amount
59	12-30-09	500.00
1	11-30-14	500.00

Amount financed	23,493.11
APR	9.9
Finance charges	6,506.89
Total of payments	30,000.00
Total sales price	30,000.00

****

Price	23,625.50
Accessories	.00
Doc fee	55.00
Dealer smog	.00
Sales tax	1,953.64
Service agreement	.00
Cash price	25,689.14

DMV fees	208.00
Insurance premiums	.00
Total purchase	25,897.14

Trade-in	.00
Less payoff	.00
Net trade-in	.00
Deferred down	.00
Amount paid now	.00
Total down payment	.00

***** Payment Schedule *****

Due / Starting		Amount
59	12-30-09	550.00
1	11-30-14	550.00

Amount financed	25,897.14
APR	9.9
Finance charges	7,102.85
Total of payments	33,000.00
Total sales price	33,000.00

Price	25,782.52	
Accessories	.00	
Doc fee	55.00	
Dealer smog	.00	
Sales tax	2,131.59	
Service agreement	.00	
Cash price	27,969.11	

***** Payment Schedule *****

Due / Starting		Amount
59	12-30-09	600.00
1	11-30-14	600.00

DMV fees	222.00
Insurance premiums	.00
Total purchase	28,191.11

Amount financed	28,191.11
APR	9.9
Finance charges	7,808.89
Total of payments	36,000.00
Total sales price	36,000.00

Trade-in	.00
Less payoff	.00
Net trade-in	.00
Deferred down	.00
Amount paid now	.00
Total down payment	.00

****

Price	27,939.66
Accessories	.00
Doc fee	55.00
Dealer smog	.00
Sales tax	2,309.55
Service agreement	.00
Cash price	30,304.21

***** Payment Schedule *****

Due / Starting		Amount
59	12-30-09	650.00
1	11-30-14	650.00

DMV fees	236.00
Insurance premiums	.00
Total purchase	30,540.21

Amount financed	30,540.21
APR	9.9
Finance charges	8,459.79
Total of payments	39,000.00
Total sales price	39,000.00

Trade-in	.00
Less payoff	.00
Net trade-in	.00
Deferred down	.00
Amount paid now	.00
Total down payment	.00

Price	30,095.75
Accessories	.00
Doc fee	55.00
Dealer smog	.00
Sales tax	2,487.43
Service agreement	.00
Cash price	32,638.18

DMV fees	251.00
Insurance premiums	.00
Total purchase	32,889.18

Trade-in	.00
Less payoff	.00
Net trade-in	.00
Deferred down	.00
Amount paid now	.00
Total down payment	.00

***** Payment Schedule *****

Due / Starting		Amount
59	12-30-09	700.00
1	11-30-14	700.00

Amount financed	32,889.18
APR	9.9
Finance charges	9,110.82
Total of payments	42,000.00
Total sales price	42,000.00

****

Price	32,198.96
Accessories	.00
Doc fee	55.00
Dealer smog	.00
Sales tax	2,660.95
Service agreement	.00
Cash price	34,914.91

DMV fees	264.00
Insurance premiums	.00
Total purchase	35,178.91

Trade-in	.00
Less payoff	.00
Net trade-in	.00
Deferred down	.00
Amount paid now	.00
Total down payment	.00

***** Payment Schedule *****

Due / Starting		Amount
59	12-30-09	750.00
1	11-30-14	750.00

Amount financed	35,178.91
APR	9.9
Finance charges	9,821.09
Total of payments	45,000.00
Total sales price	45,000.00

Price	34,355.83
Accessories	.00
Doc fee	55.00
Dealer smog	.00
Sales tax	2,838.89
Service agreement	.00
Cash price	37,249.72

DMV fees	278.00
Insurance premiums	.00
Total purchase	37,527.72

Trade-in	.00
Less payoff	.00
Net trade-in	.00
Deferred down	.00
Amount paid now	.00
Total down payment	.00

***** Payment Schedule *****

Due / Starting		Amount
59	12-30-09	800.00
1	11-30-14	800.00

Amount financed	37,527.72
APR	9.9
Finance charges	10,472.28
Total of payments	48,000.00
Total sales price	48,000.00

****

Price	36,567.59
Accessories	.00
Doc fee	55.00
Dealer smog	.00
Sales tax	3,021.36
Service agreement	.00
Cash price	39,643.95

DMV fees	292.00
Insurance premiums	.00
Total purchase	39,935.95

Trade-in	.00
Less payoff	.00
Net trade-in	.00
Deferred down	.00
Amount paid now	.00
Total down payment	.00

***** Payment Schedule *****

Due / Starting		Amount
59	12-30-09	850.00
1	11-30-14	850.00

Amount financed	39,935.95
APR	9.9
Finance charges	11,064.05
Total of payments	51,000.00
Total sales price	51,000.00

Price	38,724.06
Accessories	.00
Doc fee	55.00
Dealer smog	.00
Sales tax	3,199.27
Service agreement	.00
Cash price	41,978.33

DMV fees	307.00
Insurance premiums	.00
Total purchase	42,285.33

Trade-in	.00
Less payoff	.00
Net trade-in	.00
Deferred down	.00
Amount paid now	.00
Total down payment	.00

***** Payment Schedule *****

Due / Starting		Amount
59	12-30-09	900.00
1	11-30-14	900.00

Amount financed	42,285.33
APR	9.9
Finance charges	11,714.67
Total of payments	54,000.00
Total sales price	54,000.00

****

Price	40,881.23
Accessories	.00
Doc fee	55.00
Dealer smog	.00
Sales tax	3,377.23
Service agreement	.00
Cash price	44,313.46

DMV fees	321.00
Insurance premiums	.00
Total purchase	44,634.46

Trade-in	.00
Less payoff	.00
Net trade-in	.00
Deferred down	.00
Amount paid now	.00
Total down payment	.00

***** Payment Schedule *****

Due / Starting		Amount
59	12-30-09	950.00
1	11-30-14	950.00

Amount financed	44,634.46
APR	9.9
Finance charges	12,365.54
Total of payments	57,000.00
Total sales price	57,000.00

Price	43,037.70
Accessories	.00
Doc fee	55.00
Dealer smog	.00
Sales tax	3,555.14
Service agreement	.00
Cash price	46,647.84
DMV fees	335.00
Insurance premiums	.00
Total purchase	46,982.84
Trade-in	.00
Less payoff	.00
Net trade-in	.00
Deferred down	.00
Amount paid now	.00
Total down payment	.00

***** Payment Schedule *****

Due / Starting		Amount
59	12-30-09	1,000.00
1	11-30-14	1,000.00

Amount financed	46,982.84
APR	9.9
Finance charges	13,017.15
Total of payments	60,000.00
Total sales price	60,000.00

Dr. Smith, I took your advice about the book *Buyers vs. Liars,* and my grandson saved over $4,000 on his new dream car, and it is a beauty!

Payment Schedule Charts at 11.9% for 60 Months

Price	8,076.25
Accessories	.00
Doc fee	35.00
Dealer smog	.00
Sales tax	669.17
Service agreement	.00
Cash price	8,780.42

DMV fees	108.00
Insurance premiums	.00
Total purchase	8,888.42

Trade-in	.00
Less payoff	.00
Net trade-in	.00
Deferred down	.00
Amount paid now	.00
Total down payment	.00

***** Payment Schedule *****

Due / Starting		Amount
59	12-30-09	200.00
1	11-30-14	200.00

Amount financed	8,888.42
APR	11.9
Finance charges	3,111.58
Total of payments	12,000.00
Total sales price	12,000.00

****

Price	10,135.20
Accessories	.00
Doc fee	35.00
Dealer smog	.00
Sales tax	839.04
Service agreement	.00
Cash price	11,009.24

DMV fees	121.00
Insurance premiums	.00
Total purchase	11,130.24

Trade-in	.00
Less payoff	.00
Net trade-in	.00
Deferred down	.00
Amount paid now	.00
Total down payment	.00

***** Payment Schedule *****

Due / Starting		Amount
59	12-30-09	250.00
1	11-30-14	250.00

Amount financed	11,130.24
APR	11.9
Finance charges	3,869.76
Total of payments	15,000.00
Total sales price	15,000.00

Price	12,194.09
Accessories	.00
Doc fee	35.00
Dealer smog	29.00
Sales tax	1,011.29
Service agreement	.00
Cash price	13,268.38

***** Payment Schedule *****

Due / Starting		Amount
59	12-30-09	300.00
1	11-30-14	300.00

DMV fees	134.00
Insurance premiums	.00
Total purchase	13,403.38

Amount financed	13,403.38
APR	11.9
Finance charges	4,596.62
Total of payments	18,000.00
Total sales price	18,000.00

Trade-in	.00
Less payoff	.00
Net trade-in	.00
Deferred down	.00
Amount paid now	.00
Total down payment	.00

****

Price	14,252.12
Accessories	.00
Doc fee	35.00
Dealer smog	29.00
Sales tax	1,181.07
Service agreement	.00
Cash price	15,497.19

***** Payment Schedule *****

Due / Starting		Amount
59	12-30-09	350.00
1	11-30-14	350.00

DMV fees	148.00
Insurance premiums	.00
Total purchase	15,645.19

Amount financed	15,645.19
APR	11.9
Finance charges	5,354.81
Total of payments	21,000.00
Total sales price	21,000.00

Trade-in	.00
Less payoff	.00
Net trade-in	.00
Deferred down	.00
Amount paid now	.00
Total down payment	.00

Price	16,310.95
Accessories	.00
Doc fee	35.00
Dealer smog	29.00
Sales tax	1,350.93
Service agreement	.00
Cash price	17,725.88

***** Payment Schedule *****

Due / Starting		Amount
59	12-30-09	400.00
1	11-30-14	400.00

DMV fees	161.00
Insurance premiums	.00
Total purchase	17,886.88

Amount financed	17,886.88
APR	11.9
Finance charges	6,113.12
Total of payments	24,000.00
Total sales price	24,000.00

Trade-in	.00
Less payoff	.00
Net trade-in	.00
Deferred down	.00
Amount paid now	.00
Total down payment	.00

****

Price	18,369.84
Accessories	.00
Doc fee	35.00
Dealer smog	29.00
Sales tax	1,520.07
Service agreement	.00
Cash price	19,954.63

***** Payment Schedule *****

Due / Starting		Amount
59	12-30-09	450.00
1	11-30-14	450.00

DMV fees	174.00
Insurance premiums	.00
Total purchase	20,128.63

Amount financed	20,128.63
APR	11.9
Finance charges	6,871.37
Total of payments	27,000.00
Total sales price	27,000.00

Trade-in	.00
Less payoff	.00
Net trade-in	.00
Deferred down	.00
Amount paid now	.00
Total down payment	.00

Price	20,427.80
Accessories	.00
Doc fee	35.00
Dealer smog	29.00
Sales tax	1,690.57
Service agreement	.00
Cash price	22,182.37

DMV fees	188.00
Insurance premiums	.00
Total purchase	22,370.37

Trade-in	.00
Less payoff	.00
Net trade-in	.00
Deferred down	.00
Amount paid now	.00
Total down payment	.00

***** Payment Schedule *****

Due / Starting		Amount
59	12-30-09	500.00
1	11-30-14	500.00

Amount financed	22,370.37
APR	11.9
Finance charges	7,629.67
Total of payments	30,000.00
Total sales price	30,000.00

****

Price	22,486.69
Accessories	.00
Doc fee	35.00
Dealer smog	29.00
Sales tax	1,860.43
Service agreement	.00
Cash price	24,411.12

DMV fees	201.00
Insurance premiums	.00
Total purchase	24,612.12

Trade-in	.00
Less payoff	.00
Net trade-in	.00
Deferred down	.00
Amount paid now	.00
Total down payment	.00

***** Payment Schedule *****

Due / Starting		Amount
59	12-30-09	550.00
1	11-30-14	550.00

Amount financed	24,612.12
APR	11.9
Finance charges	8,387.88
Total of payments	33,000.00
Total sales price	33,000.00

Price	24,545.86
Accessories	.00
Doc fee	35.00
Dealer smog	29.00
Sales tax	2,030.31
Service agreement	.00
Cash price	26,640.17

DMV fees	214.00
Insurance premiums	.00
Total purchase	26,854.17

Trade-in	.00
Less payoff	.00
Net trade-in	.00
Deferred down	.00
Amount paid now	.00
Total down payment	.00

***** Payment Schedule *****

Due / Starting		Amount
59	12-30-09	600.00
1	11-30-14	600.00

Amount financed	26,854.17
APR	11.9
Finance charges	9,145.83
Total of payments	36,000.00
Total sales price	36,000.00

****

Price	26,657.77
Accessories	.00
Doc fee	35.00
Dealer smog	29.00
Sales tax	2,204.54
Service agreement	.00
Cash price	28,926.31

DMV fees	229.00
Insurance premiums	.00
Total purchase	29,155.31

Less payoff	.00
Net trade-in	.00
Deferred down	.00
Amount paid now	.00
Total down payment	.00

***** Payment Schedule *****

Due / Starting		Amount
59	12-30-09	650.00
1	11-30-14	650.00

Amount financed	29,155.31
APR	11.9
Finance charges	9,844.69
Total of payments	39,000.00
Total sales price	39,000.00

Price	28,661.54
Accessories	.00
Doc fee	35.00
Dealer smog	29.00
Sales tax	2,369.85
Service agreement	.00
Cash price	31,095.39

DMV fees	242.00
Insurance premiums	.00
Total purchase	31,337.39

Trade-in	.00
Less payoff	.00
Net trade-in	.00
Deferred down	.00
Amount paid now	.00
Total down payment	.00

***** Payment Schedule *****

Due / Starting		Amount
59	12-30-09	700.00
1	11-30-14	700.00

Amount financed	31,337.39
APR	11.9
Finance charges	10.663.61
Total of payments	42,000.00
Total sales price	42,000.00

****

Price	30,720.65
Accessories	.00
Doc fee	35.00
Dealer smog	29.00
Sales tax	2,539.73
Service agreement	.00
Cash price	33,324.38

DMV fees	255.00
Insurance premiums	.00
Total purchase	33,579.38

Trade-in	.00
Less payoff	.00
Net trade-in	.00
Deferred down	.00
Amount paid now	.00
Total down payment	.00

***** Payment Schedule *****

Due / Starting		Amount
59	12-30-09	750.00
1	11-30-14	750.00

Amount financed	33,579.38
APR	11.9
Finance charges	11,420.62
Total of payments	45,000.00
Total sales price	45,000.00

Price	32,779.32
Accessories	.00
Doc fee	35.00
Dealer smog	29.00
Sales tax	2,709.57
Service agreement	.00
Cash price	35,552.89

DMV fees	268.00
Insurance premiums	.00
Total purchase	35,820.89

Trade-in	.00
Less payoff	.00
Net trade-in	.00
Deferred down	.00
Amount paid now	.00
Total down payment	.00

***** Payment Schedule *****

Due / Starting		Amount
59	12-30-09	800.00
1	11-30-14	800.00

Amount financed	35,820.89
APR	11.9
Finance charges	12,179.11
Total of payments	48,000.00
Total sales price	48,000.00

****

Price	34,837.29
Accessories	.00
Doc fee	35.00
Dealer smog	29.00
Sales tax	2,879.35
Service agreement	.00
Cash price	37,780.64

DMV fees	282.00
Insurance premiums	.00
Total purchase	38,062.64

Trade-in	.00
Less payoff	.00
Net trade-in	.00
Deferred down	.00
Amount paid now	.00
Total down payment	.00

***** Payment Schedule *****

Due / Starting		Amount
59	12-30-09	850.00
1	11-30-14	850.00

Amount financed	38,062.64
APR	11.9
Finance charges	12,937.36
Total of payments	51,000.00
Total sales price	51,000.00

Price	36,896.18
Accessories	.00
Doc fee	35.00
Dealer smog	29.00
Sales tax	3,049.21
Service agreement	.00
Cash price	40,009.39
DMV fees	295.00
Insurance premiums	.00
Total purchase	40,304.39
Trade-in	.00
Less payoff	.00
Net trade-in	.00
Deferred down	.00
Amount paid now	.00
Total down payment	.00

***** Payment Schedule *****

Due / Starting		Amount
59	12-30-09	900.00
1	11-30-14	900.00

Amount financed	40,304.39
APR	11.9
Finance charges	13,695.61
Total of payments	54,000.00
Total sales price	54,000.00

****

Price	38,955.07
Accessories	.00
Doc fee	35.00
Dealer smog	29.00
Sales tax	3,219.07
Service agreement	.00
Cash price	42,238.14
DMV fees	308.00
Insurance premiums	.00
Total purchase	42,546.14
Trade-in	.00
Less payoff	.00
Net trade-in	.00
Deferred down	.00
Amount paid now	.00
Total down payment	.00

***** Payment Schedule *****

Due / Starting		Amount
59	12-30-09	950.00
1	11-30-14	950.00

Amount financed	42,546.14
APR	11.9
Finance charges	14,453.86
Total of payments	57,000.00
Total sales price	57,000.00

Price	41,012.96
Accessories	.00
Doc fee	35.00
Dealer smog	29.00
Sales tax	3,388.84
Service agreement	.00
Cash price	44,465.80
DMV fees	322.00
Insurance premiums	.00
Total purchase	44,788.80
Trade-in	.00
Less payoff	.00
Net trade-in	.00
Deferred down	.00
Amount paid now	.00
Total down payment	.00

***** Payment Schedule *****

Due / Starting		Amount
59	12-30-09	1,000.00
1	11-30-14	1,000.00

Amount financed	44,788.80
APR	11.9
Finance charges	15,512.20
Total of payments	60,000.00
Total sales price	60,000.00

Did everyone see how the dealers tried to trick the public with their advertisement? Remember, we are the next generation of buying citizens! This is a great book! Remember to fight for the price.

Payment Schedule Charts at 13.9% for 60 Months

Price	7,870.86
Accessories	.00
Doc fee	35.00
Dealer smog	.00
Sales tax	652.23
Service agreement	.00
Cash price	8,558.09

***** Payment Schedule *****

Due / Starting		Amount
59	12-30-09	200.00
1	11-30-14	200.00

DMV fees	106.00
Insurance premiums	.00
Total purchase	8,664.09

Amount financed	8,664.09
APR	13.9
Finance charges	3,335.91
Total of payments	12,000.00
Total sales price	12,000.00

Trade-in	.00
Less payoff	.00
Net trade-in	.00
Deferred down	.00
Amount paid now	.00
Total down payment	.00

****

Price	9,878.05
Accessories	.00
Doc fee	35.00
Dealer smog	29.00
Sales tax	820.21
Service agreement	.00
Cash price	10,762.26

***** Payment Schedule *****

Due / Starting		Amount
59	12-30-09	250.00
1	11-30-14	250.00

DMV fees	119.00
Insurance premiums	.00
Total purchase	10,881.26

Amount financed	10,881.26
APR	13.9
Finance charges	4,118.74
Total of payments	15,000.00
Total sales price	15,000.00

Trade-in	.00
Less payoff	.00
Net trade-in	.00
Deferred down	.00
Amount paid now	.00
Total down payment	.00

Price	11,885.07
Accessories	.00
Doc fee	35.00
Dealer smog	29.00
Sales tax	985.79
Service agreement	.00
Cash price	12,934.86

DMV fees	132.00
Insurance premiums	.00
Total purchase	13,066.86

Trade-in	.00
Less payoff	.00
Net trade-in	.00
Deferred down	.00
Amount paid now	.00
Total down payment	.00

***** Payment Schedule *****

Due / Starting		Amount
59	12-30-09	300.00
1	11-30-14	300.00

Amount financed	13,066.86
APR	13.9
Finance charges	4,933.14
Total of payments	18,000.00
Total sales price	18,000.00

****

Price	13,892.15
Accessories	.00
Doc fee	35.00
Dealer smog	29.00
Sales tax	1,150.64
Service agreement	.00
Cash price	15,106.79

DMV fees	145.00
Insurance premiums	.00
Total purchase	15,251.79

Trade-in	.00
Less payoff	.00
Net trade-in	.00
Deferred down	.00
Amount paid now	.00
Total down payment	.00

***** Payment Schedule *****

Due / Starting		Amount
59	12-30-09	350.00
1	11-30-14	350.00

Amount financed	15,251.79
APR	13.9
Finance charges	5,748.21
Total of payments	21,000.00
Total sales price	21,000.00

Price	15,899.32
Accessories	.00
Doc fee	35.00
Dealer smog	29.00
Sales tax	1,316.97
Service agreement	.00
Cash price	17,280.29

DMV fees	158.00
Insurance premiums	.00
Total purchase	17,438.20

Trade-in	.00
Less payoff	.00
Net trade-in	.00
Deferred down	.00
Amount paid now	.00
Total down payment	.00

***** Payment Schedule *****

Due / Starting		Amount
59	12-30-09	400.00
1	11-30-14	400.00

Amount financed	17,438.20
APR	13.9
Finance charges	6,561.80
Total of payments	24,000.00
Total sales price	24,000.00

****

Price	17,906.39
Accessories	.00
Doc fee	35.00
Dealer smog	29.00
Sales tax	1,482.55
Service agreement	.00
Cash price	19,452.94

DMV fees	171.00
Insurance premiums	.00
Total purchase	19,623.94

Trade-in	.00
Less payoff	.00
Net trade-in	.00
Deferred down	.00
Amount paid now	.00
Total down payment	.00

***** Payment Schedule *****

Due / Starting		Amount
59	12-30-09	450.00
1	11-30-14	450.00

Amount financed	19,623.94
APR	13.9
Finance charges	7,376.06
Total of payments	27,000.00
Total sales price	27,000.00

Price	19,913.62
Accessories	.00
Doc fee	35.00
Dealer smog	29.00
Sales tax	1,648.15
Service agreement	.00
Cash price	21,625.77

DMV fees	184.00
Insurance premiums	.00
Total purchase	21,809.77

Trade-in	.00
Less payoff	.00
Net trade-in	.00
Deferred down	.00
Amount paid now	.00
Total down payment	.00

***** Payment Schedule *****

Due / Starting		Amount
59	12-30-09	500.00
1	11-30-14	500.00

Amount financed	21,809.77
APR	13.9
Finance charges	8,190.23
Total of payments	30,000.00
Total sales price	30,000.00

****

Price	21,920.48
Accessories	.00
Doc fee	35.00
Dealer smog	29.00
Sales tax	1,813.71
Service agreement	.00
Cash price	23,798.19

DMV fees	197.00
Insurance premiums	.00
Total purchase	23,995.19

Trade-in	.00
Less payoff	.00
Net trade-in	.00
Deferred down	.00
Amount paid now	.00
Total down payment	.00

***** Payment Schedule *****

Due / Starting		Amount
59	12-30-09	550.00
1	11-30-14	550.00

Amount financed	23,995.19
APR	13.9
Finance charges	9,004.81
Total of payments	33,000.00
Total sales price	33,000.00

Price	23,927.63	***** Payment Schedule *****	
Accessories	.00		
Doc fee	35.00	Due / Starting	Amount
Dealer smog	29.00		
Sales tax	1,979.30		
Service agreement	.00	59 12-30-09	600.00
Cash price	25,970.93	1 11-30-14	600.00
DMV fees	210.00	Amount financed	26,180.93
Insurance premiums	.00	APR	13.9
Total purchase	26,180.93	Finance charges	9,819.07
		Total of payments	36,000.00
		Total sales price	36,000.00
Trade-in	.00		
Less payoff	.00		
Net trade-in	.00		
Deferred down	.00		
Amount paid now	.00		
Total down payment	.00		

****

Price	25,934.70	***** Payment Schedule *****	
Accessories	.00		
Doc fee	35.00	Due / Starting	Amount
Dealer smog	29.00		
Sales tax	2,144.89		
Service agreement	.00	59 12-30-09	650.00
Cash price	28,143.59	1 11-30-14	650.00
DMV fees	223.00	Amount financed	28,366.59
Insurance premiums	.00	APR	13.9
Total purchase	28,366.59	Finance charges	10,633.41
		Total of payments	39,000.00
		Total sales price	39,000.00
Trade-in	.00		
Less payoff	.00		
Net trade-in	.00		
Deferred down	.00		
Amount paid now	.00		
Total down payment	.00		

Price	27,941.73
Accessories	.00
Doc fee	35.00
Dealer smog	29.00
Sales tax	2,310.47
Service agreement	.00
Cash price	30,316.20

DMV fees	236.00
Insurance premiums	.00
Total purchase	30,552.20

Trade-in	.00
Less payoff	.00
Net trade-in	.00
Deferred down	.00
Amount paid now	.00
Total down payment	.00

***** Payment Schedule *****

Due / Starting		Amount
59	12-30-09	700.00
1	11-30-14	700.00

Amount financed	30,552.20
APR	13.9
Finance charges	11,447.80
Total of payments	42,000.00
Total sales price	42,000.00

****

Price	29,948.84
Accessories	.00
Doc fee	35.00
Dealer smog	29.00
Sales tax	2,476.05
Service agreement	.00
Cash price	32,488.89

DMV fees	249.00
Insurance premiums	.00
Total purchase	33,737.89

Trade-in	.00
Less payoff	.00
Net trade-in	.00
Deferred down	.00
Amount paid now	.00
Total down payment	.00

***** Payment Schedule *****

Due / Starting		Amount
59	12-30-09	750.00
1	11-30-14	750.00

Amount financed	33,737.89
APR	13.9
Finance charges	12,262.11
Total of payments	45,000.00
Total sales price	45,000.00

Price	31,955.98	***** Payment Schedule *****	
Accessories	.00		
Doc fee	35.00	Due / Starting	Amount
Dealer smog	29.00		
Sales tax	2,641.64		
Service agreement	.00	59 12-30-09	800.00
Cash price	34,661.62	1 11-30-14	800.00
DMV fees	262.00	Amount financed	34,923.62
Insurance premiums	.00	APR	13.9
Total purchase	34,923.62	Finance charges	13,076.38
		Total of payments	48,000.00
		Total sales price	48,000.00
Trade-in	.00		
Less payoff	.00		
Net trade-in	.00		
Deferred down	.00		
Amount paid now	.00		
Total down payment	.00		

****

Price	33,962.97	***** Payment Schedule *****	
Accessories	.00		
Doc fee	35.00	Due / Starting	Amount
Dealer smog	29.00		
Sales tax	2,807.22		
Service agreement	.00	59 12-30-09	850.00
Cash price	36,834.19	1 11-30-14	850.00
DMV fees	275.00	Amount financed	37,109.19
Insurance premiums	.00	APR	13.9
Total purchase	37,109.19	Finance charges	13,890.81
		Total of payments	51,000.00
		Total sales price	51,000.00
Trade-in	.00		
Less payoff	.00		
Net trade-in	.00		
Deferred down	.00		
Amount paid now	.00		
Total down payment	.00		

Price	35,970.05
Accessories	.00
Doc fee	35.00
Dealer smog	29.00
Sales tax	2,972.80
Service agreement	.00
Cash price	39,006.85

***** Payment Schedule *****

Due / Starting		Amount
59	12-30-09	900.00
1	11-30-14	900.00

DMV fees	288.00
Insurance premiums	.00
Total purchase	39,294.85

Amount financed	39,294.85
APR	13.9
Finance charges	14,705.15
Total of payments	54,000.00
Total sales price	54,000.00

Trade-in	.00
Less payoff	.00
Net trade-in	.00
Deferred down	.00
Amount paid now	.00
Total down payment	.00

****

Price	37,971.20
Accessories	.00
Doc fee	35.00
Dealer smog	29.00
Sales tax	3,137.90
Service agreement	.00
Cash price	41,173.10

***** Payment Schedule *****

Due / Starting		Amount
59	12-30-09	950.00
1	11-30-14	950.00

DMV fees	301.00
Insurance premiums	.00
Total purchase	41,474.10

Amount financed	41,474.10
APR	13.9
Finance charges	15,525.90
Total of payments	57,000.00
Total sales price	57,000.00

Trade-in	.00
Less payoff	.00
Net trade-in	.00
Deferred down	.00
Amount paid now	.00
Total down payment	.00

Price	39,984.22
Accessories	.00
Doc fee	35.00
Dealer smog	29.00
Sales tax	3,303.97
Service agreement	.00
Cash price	43,352.19

DMV fees	314.00
Insurance premiums	.00
Total purchase	43,666.19

Trade-in	.00
Less payoff	.00
Net trade-in	.00
Deferred down	.00
Amount paid now	.00
Total down payment	.00

***** Payment Schedule *****

Due / Starting		Amount
59	12-30-09	1,000.00
1	11-30-14	1,000.00

Amount financed	43,666.19
APR	13.9
Finance charges	16,333.81
Total of payments	60,000.00
Total sales price	60,000.00

Americans are having a hard time staying in their homes, due to bad loans and crooked mortgage brokers. Many foreclosed homes have caused our economy to fall along with the stock market. Let's build a newer, stronger, and honest America. *Buyers vs. Liars* will force dealerships to be fair and honest with their customers because it affects all of us.

Special Financing Department

You Will Pay 15%, 17%, or 19%

    These are customers who the dealership really take advantage of because of their credit. These consumers have little or no choice but to fight for the price. But she can, if she doesn't purchase too much vehicle. She should try to keep her monthly payments around $250 to $300 if she is single.

    With this so-called "special financing," the bank usually requires a 15% down payment of the total purchase price, including tax, license and other fees. The dealer always makes it seem like the customer must pay separately. Only 10% down or sometimes $0 down is usually required for buyers who have purchased vehicles before.

Payment Schedule Charts at 15.9% for 60 Months

Price	7,417.29
Accessories	.00
Doc fee	35.00
Dealer smog	.00
Sales tax	614.81
Service agreement	.00
Cash price	8,067.10

***** Payment Schedule *****

Due / Starting		Amount
59	12-30-09	200.00
1	11-30-14	200.00

DMV fees	104.00
Insurance premiums	.00
Total purchase	8,171.10

Amount financed	8,171.10
APR	15.9
Finance charges	3,828.90
Total of payments	12,000.00
Total sales price	12,000.00

Trade-in	.00
Less payoff	.00
Net trade-in	.00
Deferred down	.00
Amount paid now	.00
Total down payment	.00

****

Price	9,296.34
Accessories	.00
Doc fee	35.00
Dealer smog	.00
Sales tax	769.83
Service agreement	.00
Cash price	10,101.17

***** Payment Schedule *****

Due / Starting		Amount
59	12-30-09	250.00
1	11-30-14	250.00

DMV fees	117.00
Insurance premiums	.00
Total purchase	10,218.29

Amount financed	10,218.29
APR	15.9
Finance charges	4,781.71
Total of payments	15,000.00
Total sales price	15,000.00

Trade-in	.00
Less payoff	.00
Net trade-in	.00
Deferred down	.00
Amount paid now	.00
Total down payment	.00

Price	11,176.30
Accessories	.00
Doc fee	35.00
Dealer smog	.00
Sales tax	924.93
Service agreement	.00
Cash price	12,136.23

***** Payment Schedule *****

Due / Starting		Amount
59	12-30-09	300.00
1	11-30-14	300.00

DMV fees	128.00
Insurance premiums	.00
Total purchase	12,264.23

Amount financed	12,264.23
APR	15.9
Finance charges	5,735.77
Total of payments	18,000.00
Total sales price	18,000.00

Trade-in	.00
Less payoff	.00
Net trade-in	.00
Deferred down	.00
Amount paid now	.00
Total down payment	.00

****

Price	13,055.28
Accessories	.00
Doc fee	35.00
Dealer smog	.00
Sales tax	1,079.94
Service agreement	.00
Cash price	14,170.22

***** Payment Schedule *****

Due / Starting		Amount
59	12-30-09	350.00
1	11-30-14	350.00

DMV fees	140.00
Insurance premiums	.00
Total purchase	14,310.22

Amount financed	14,310.22
APR	15.9
Finance charges	6,689.78
Total of payments	21,000.00
Total sales price	21,000.00

Trade-in	.00
Less payoff	.00
Net trade-in	.00
Deferred down	.00
Amount paid now	.00
Total down payment	.00

Price	15,187.11
Accessories	.00
Doc fee	35.00
Dealer smog	.00
Sales tax	1,255.82
Service agreement	.00
Cash price	16,477.93

DMV fees	153.00
Insurance premiums	.00
Total purchase	16,630.93

Trade-in	.00
Less payoff	.00
Net trade-in	.00
Deferred down	.00
Amount paid now	.00
Total down payment	.00

***** Payment Schedule *****

Due / Starting		Amount
59	12-30-09	400.00
1	11-30-14	400.00

Amount financed	16,630.93
APR	15.9
Finance charges	7,360.07
Total of payments	24,000.00
Total sales price	24,000.00

****

Price	16,815.18
Accessories	.00
Doc fee	35.00
Dealer smog	.00
Sales tax	1,390.13
Service agreement	.00
Cash price	18,240.31

DMV fees	164.00
Insurance premiums	.00
Total purchase	18,404.31

Trade-in	.00
Less payoff	.00
Net trade-in	.00
Deferred down	.00
Amount paid now	.00
Total down payment	.00

***** Payment Schedule *****

Due / Starting		Amount
59	12-30-09	450.00
1	11-30-14	450.00

Amount financed	18,404.31
APR	15.9
Finance charges	8,595.69
Total of payments	27,000.00
Total sales price	27,000.00

Price	17,104.40	******* Payment Schedule *******	
Accessories	.00		
Doc fee	35.00	**Due / Starting**	**Amount**
Dealer smog	.00		
Sales tax	1,414.00		
Service agreement	.00	59 12-30-09	500.00
Cash price	18,553.40	1 11-30-14	500.00
DMV fees	177.00	**Amount financed**	18,730.40
Insurance premiums	.00	**APR**	15.9
Total purchase	18,730.40	**Finance charges**	11,269.60
		Total of payments	30,000.00
		Total sales price	30,000.00
Trade-in	.00		
Less payoff	.00		
Net trade-in	.00		
Deferred down	.00		
Amount paid now	.00		
Total down payment	.00		

****

Price	18,829.82	******* Payment Schedule *******	
Accessories	.00		
Doc fee	35.00	**Due / Starting**	**Amount**
Dealer smog	.00		
Sales tax	1,556.34		
Service agreement	.00	59 12-30-09	550.00
Cash price	20,421.16	1 11-30-14	550.00
DMV fees	188.00	**Amount financed**	20,609.16
Insurance premiums	.00	**APR**	15.9
Total purchase	20,609.16	**Finance charges**	12,390.84
		Total of payments	33,000.00
		Total sales price	33,000.00
Trade-in	.00		
Less payoff	.00		
Net trade-in	.00		
Deferred down	.00		
Amount paid now	.00		
Total down payment	.00		

Price	20,582.41	
Accessories	.00	
Doc fee	35.00	
Dealer smog	.00	
Sales tax	1,698.83	
Service agreement	.00	
Cash price	22,290.81	

***** Payment Schedule *****

Due / Starting		Amount
59	12-30-09	600.00
1	11-30-14	600.00

DMV fees	188.00	
Insurance premiums	.00	
Total purchase	22,478.81	

Amount financed	22,478.81
APR	15.9
Finance charges	13,521.19
Total of payments	36,000.00
Total sales price	36,000.00

Trade-in	.00
Less payoff	.00
Net trade-in	.00
Deferred down	.00
Amount paid now	.00
Total down payment	.00

****

Price	22,282.41	
Accessories	.00	
Doc fee	35.00	
Dealer smog	.00	
Sales tax	1,841.18	
Service agreement	.00	
Cash price	24,158.59	

***** Payment Schedule *****

Due / Starting		Amount
59	12-30-09	650.00
1	11-30-14	650.00

DMV fees	200.00	
Insurance premiums	.00	
Total purchase	24,358.59	

Amount financed	24,358.59
APR	15.9
Finance charges	14,641.41
Total of payments	39,000.00
Total sales price	39,000.00

Trade-in	.00
Less payoff	.00
Net trade-in	.00
Deferred down	.00
Amount paid now	.00
Total down payment	.00

Price	24,007.82
Accessories	.00
Doc fee	35.00
Dealer smog	.00
Sales tax	1,983.53
Service agreement	.00
Cash price	26,026.35

DMV fees	212.00
Insurance premiums	.00
Total purchase	26,238.35

Trade-in	.00
Less payoff	.00
Net trade-in	.00
Deferred down	.00
Amount paid now	.00
Total down payment	.00

***** Payment Schedule *****

Due / Starting		Amount
59	12-30-09	700.00
1	11-30-14	700.00

Amount financed	26,238.35
APR	15.9
Finance charges	15,761.65
Total of payments	42,000.00
Total sales price	42,000.00

****

Price	25,677.93
Accessories	.00
Doc fee	35.00
Dealer smog	.00
Sales tax	2,123.31
Service agreement	.00
Cash price	27,836.24

DMV fees	222.00
Insurance premiums	.00
Total purchase	28,058.24

Trade-in	.00
Less payoff	.00
Net trade-in	.00
Deferred down	.00
Amount paid now	.00
Total down payment	.00

***** Payment Schedule *****

Due / Starting		Amount
59	12-30-09	750.00
1	11-30-14	750.00

Amount financed	28,058.24
APR	15.9
Finance charges	16,941.76
Total of payments	45,000.00
Total sales price	45,000.00

Price	27,399.41
Accessories	.00
Doc fee	35.00
Dealer smog	.00
Sales tax	2,263.33
Service agreement	.00
Cash price	29,697.74
DMV fees	232.00
Insurance premiums	.00
Total purchase	29,929.74
Trade-in	.00
Less payoff	.00
Net trade-in	.00
Deferred down	.00
Amount paid now	.00
Total down payment	.00

***** Payment Schedule *****

Due / Starting		Amount
59	12-30-09	800.00
1	11-30-14	800.00

Amount financed	29,929.74
APR	15.9
Finance charges	18,070.26
Total of payments	48,000.00
Total sales price	48,000.00

****

Price	29,122.91
Accessories	.00
Doc fee	35.00
Dealer smog	.00
Sales tax	2,404.52
Service agreement	.00
Cash price	31,562.43
DMV fees	244.00
Insurance premiums	.00
Total purchase	31,806.43
Trade-in	.00
Less payoff	.00
Net trade-in	.00
Deferred down	.00
Amount paid now	.00
Total down payment	.00

***** Payment Schedule *****

Due / Starting		Amount
59	12-30-09	850.00
1	11-30-14	850.00

Amount financed	31,806.43
APR	15.9
Finance charges	19,193.73
Total of payments	51,000.00
Total sales price	51,000.00

Price	30,844.56
Accessories	.00
Doc fee	35.00
Dealer smog	.00
Sales tax	2,547.56
Service agreement	.00
Cash price	33,427.12

DMV fees	256.00
Insurance premiums	.00
Total purchase	33,683.12

Trade-in	.00
Less payoff	.00
Net trade-in	.00
Deferred down	.00
Amount paid now	.00
Total down payment	.00

***** Payment Schedule *****

Due / Starting		Amount
59	12-30-09	900.00
1	11-30-14	900.00

Amount financed	33,683.12
APR	15.9
Finance charges	20,316.88
Total of payments	54,000.00
Total sales price	54,000.00

****

Price	32,568.06
Accessories	.00
Doc fee	35.00
Dealer smog	.00
Sales tax	2,689.75
Service agreement	.00
Cash price	35,292.81

DMV fees	266.00
Insurance premiums	.00
Total purchase	35,558.81

Trade-in	.00
Less payoff	.00
Net trade-in	.00
Deferred down	.00
Amount paid now	.00
Total down payment	.00

***** Payment Schedule *****

Due / Starting		Amount
59	12-30-09	950.00
1	11-30-14	950.00

Amount financed	35,558.81
APR	15.9
Finance charges	21,441.19
Total of payments	57,000.00
Total sales price	57,000.00

Price	34,289.60
Accessories	.00
Doc fee	35.00
Dealer smog	.00
Sales tax	2,831.77
Service agreement	.00
Cash price	37,156.37

DMV fees	278.00
Insurance premiums	.00
Total purchase	37,434.37

Trade-in	.00
Less payoff	.00
Net trade-in	.00
Deferred down	.00
Amount Paid Now	.00
Total down payment	.00

***** Payment Schedule *****

Due / Starting		Amount
59	12-30-09	1,000.00
1	11-30-14	1,000.00

Amount financed	37,434.37
APR	15.9
Finance charges	22,565.63
Total of payments	60,000.00
Total sales price	60,000.00

This book, *Buyers vs. Liars*, has my entire family saving on their monthly payments when they purchased their new vehicles. Saving extra money helps!

Payment Schedule Chart at 17.9% for 60 Months

Price	7,022.20
Accessories	.00
Doc fee	35.00
Dealer smog	.00
Sales tax	582.21
Service agreement	.00
Cash price	7,639.41

***** Payment Schedule *****

Due / Starting		Amount
59	12-30-09	200.00
1	11-30-14	200.00

DMV fees	101.00
Insurance premiums	.00
Total purchase	7,749.41

Amount financed	7,749.41
APR	17.9
Finance charges	4, 259.59
Total of payments	12,000.00
Total sales price	12,000.00

Trade-in	.00
Less payoff	.00
Net trade-in	.00
Deferred down	.00
Amount paid now	.00
Total down payment	.00

****

Price	8,816.77
Accessories	.00
Doc fee	35.00
Dealer smog	.00
Sales tax	730.27
Service agreement	.00
Cash price	9,582.04

***** Payment Schedule *****

Due / Starting		Amount
59	12-30-09	250.00
1	11-30-14	250.00

DMV fees	113.00
Insurance premiums	.00
Total purchase	9,695.04

Amount financed	9,695.04
APR	17.9
Finance charges	5,304.96
Total of payments	15,000.00
Total sales price	15,000.00

Trade-in	.00
Less payoff	.00
Net trade-in	.00
Deferred down	.00
Amount paid now	.00
Total down payment	.00

Price	10,611.47	
Accessories	.00	
Doc fee	35.00	
Dealer smog	.00	
Sales tax	878.33	
Service agreement	.00	
Cash price	11,524.80	

***** Payment Schedule *****

Due / Starting		Amount
59	12-30-09	300.00
1	11-30-14	300.00

DMV fees	125.00
Insurance premiums	.00
Total purchase	11,649.80

Amount financed	11,649.80
APR	17.9
Finance charges	6,350.20
Total of payments	18,000.00
Total sales price	18,000.00

Trade-in	.00
Less payoff	.00
Net trade-in	.00
Deferred down	.00
Amount paid now	.00
Total down payment	.00

****

Price	12,406.84
Accessories	.00
Doc fee	35.00
Dealer smog	.00
Sales tax	1,023.56
Service agreement	.00
Cash price	13,465.40

***** Payment Schedule *****

Due / Starting		Amount
59	12-30-09	350.00
1	11-30-14	350.00

DMV fees	136.00
Insurance premiums	.00
Total purchase	13,601.40

Amount financed	13,601.40
APR	17.9
Finance charges	7,398.60
Total of payments	21,000.00
Total sales price	21,000.00

Trade-in	.00
Less payoff	.00
Net trade-in	.00
Deferred down	.00
Amount paid now	.00
Total down payment	.00

Price	14,201.58
Accessories	.00
Doc fee	35.00
Dealer smog	.00
Sales tax	1,174.51
Service agreement	.00
Cash price	15,411.09

DMV fees	148.00
Insurance premiums	.00
Total purchase	15,559.09

Trade-in	.00
Less payoff	.00
Net trade-in	.00
Deferred down	.00
Amount paid now	.00
Total down payment	.00

***** Payment Schedule *****

Due / Starting		Amount
59	12-30-09	400.00
1	11-30-14	400.00

Amount financed	15,559.09
APR	17.9
Finance charges	8,440.91
Total of payments	24,000.00
Total sales price	24,000.00

****

Price	15,998.06
Accessories	.00
Doc fee	35.00
Dealer smog	.00
Sales tax	1,322.72
Service agreement	.00
Cash price	17,355.78

DMV fees	158.00
Insurance premiums	.00
Total purchase	17,513.78

Trade-in	.00
Less payoff	.00
Net trade-in	.00
Deferred down	.00
Amount paid now	.00
Total down payment	.00

***** Payment Schedule *****

Due / Starting		Amount
59	12-30-09	450.00
1	11-30-14	450.00

Amount financed	17,513.78
APR	17.9
Finance charges	9,486.22
Total of payments	27,000.00
Total sales price	27,000.00

		***** Payment Schedule *****	
Price	17,792.68		
Accessories	.00		
Doc fee	35.00	Due / Starting	Amount
Dealer smog	.00		
Sales tax	1,470.78		
Service agreement	.00	59 12-30-09	500.00
Cash price	19,298.46	1 11-30-14	500.00
DMV fees	170.00	Amount financed	19,468.46
Insurance premiums	.00	APR	17.9
Total purchase	19,468.46	Finance charges	10, 531.54
		Total of payments	30,000.00
		Total sales price	30,000.00
Trade-in	.00		
Less payoff	.00		
Net trade-in	.00		
Deferred down	.00		
Amount paid now	.00		
Total down payment	.00		

****

		***** Payment Schedule *****	
Price	19,587.32		
Accessories	.00		
Doc fee	35.00	Due / Starting	Amount
Dealer smog	.00		
Sales tax	1,618.84		
Service agreement	.00	59 12-30-09	550.00
Cash price	21,241.16	1 11-30-14	550.00
DMV fees	182.00	Amount financed	21,423.16
Insurance premiums	.00	APR	17.9
Total purchase	21,423.16	Finance charges	11,576.84
		Total of payments	33,000.00
		Total sales price	33,000.00
Trade-in	.00		
Less payoff	.00		
Net trade-in	.00		
Deferred down	.00		
Amount paid now	.00		
Total down payment	.00		

Price	21,382.88	
Accessories	.00	
Doc fee	35.00	
Dealer smog	.00	
Sales tax	1,766.97	
Service agreement	.00	
Cash price	23,184.85	

***** Payment Schedule *****

Due / Starting		Amount
59	12-30-09	600.00
1	11-30-14	600.00

DMV fees	193.00
Insurance premiums	.00
Total purchase	23,377.85

Amount financed	23,377.85
APR	17.9
Finance charges	12,622.15
Total of payments	36,000.00
Total sales price	36,000.00

Trade-in	.00
Less payoff	.00
Net trade-in	.00
Deferred down	.00
Amount paid now	.00
Total down payment	.00

****

Price	23,177.52	
Accessories	.00	
Doc fee	35.00	
Dealer smog	.00	
Sales tax	1,915.03	
Service agreement	.00	
Cash price	25,127.55	

***** Payment Schedule *****

Due / Starting		Amount
59	12-30-09	650.00
1	11-30-14	650.00

DMV fees	205.00
Insurance premiums	.00
Total purchase	25,332.55

Amount financed	25,332.55
APR	17.9
Finance charges	13,667.45
Total of payments	39,000.00
Total sales price	39,000.00

Trade-in	.00
Less payoff	.00
Net trade-in	.00
Deferred down	.00
Amount paid now	.00
Total down payment	.00

Price	24,972.16
Accessories	.00
Doc fee	35.00
Dealer smog	.00
Sales tax	2,063.09
Service agreement	.00
Cash price	27,070.25

***** Payment Schedule *****

Due / Starting		Amount
59	12-30-09	700.00
1	11-30-14	700.00

DMV fees	217.00
Insurance premiums	.00
Total purchase	27,287.25

Amount financed	27,287.25
APR	17.9
Finance charges	14,712.75
Total of payments	42,000.00
Total sales price	42,000.00

Trade-in	.00
Less payoff	.00
Net trade-in	.00
Deferred down	.00
Amount paid now	.00
Total down payment	.00

****

Price	26,766.86
Accessories	.00
Doc fee	35.00
Dealer smog	.00
Sales tax	2,211.15
Service agreement	.00
Cash price	29,013.01

***** Payment Schedule *****

Due / Starting		Amount
59	12-30-09	750.00
1	11-30-14	750.00

DMV fees	229.00
Insurance premiums	.00
Total purchase	29,242.01

Amount financed	29,242.01
APR	17.9
Finance charges	15,757.99
Total of payments	45,000.00
Total sales price	45,000.00

Trade-in	.00
Less payoff	.00
Net trade-in	.00
Deferred down	.00
Amount paid now	.00
Total down payment	.00

Price	28,562.42
Accessories	.00
Doc fee	35.00
Dealer smog	.00
Sales tax	2,359.28
Service agreement	.00
Cash price	30,956.70
DMV fees	240.00
Insurance premiums	.00
Total purchase	31,196.70
Trade-in	.00
Less payoff	.00
Net trade-in	.00
Deferred down	.00
Amount paid now	.00
Total down payment	.00

***** Payment Schedule *****

Due / Starting		Amount
59	12-30-09	800.00
1	11-30-14	800.00

Amount financed	31,196.70
APR	17.9
Finance charges	16,803.30
Total of payments	48,000.00
Total sales price	48,000.00

****

Price	30,357.06
Accessories	.00
Doc fee	35.00
Dealer smog	.00
Sales tax	2,507.34
Service agreement	.00
Cash price	32,899.40
DMV fees	252.00
Insurance premiums	.00
Total purchase	33,151.40
Trade-in	.00
Less payoff	.00
Net trade-in	.00
Deferred down	.00
Amount paid now	.00
Total down payment	.00

***** Payment Schedule *****

Due / Starting		Amount
59	12-30-09	850.00
1	11-30-14	850.00

Amount financed	33,151.40
APR	17.9
Finance charges	17,848.60
Total of payments	51,000.00
Total sales price	51,000.00

Price	32,151.72	
Accessories	.00	
Doc fee	35.00	
Dealer smog	.00	
Sales tax	2,655.40	
Service agreement	.00	
Cash price	34,842.12	

***** Payment Schedule *****

Due / Starting		Amount
59	12-30-09	900.00
1	11-30-14	900.00

DMV fees	265.00
Insurance premiums	.00
Total purchase	35,107.12

Amount financed	35,107.12
APR	17.9
Finance charges	18,892.88
Total of payments	54,000.00
Total sales price	54,000.00

Trade-in	.00
Less payoff	.00
Net trade-in	.00
Deferred down	.00
Amount paid now	.00
Total down payment	.00

****

Price	33,947.25
Accessories	.00
Doc fee	35.00
Dealer smog	.00
Sales tax	2,803.53
Service agreement	.00
Cash price	36,785.78

***** Payment Schedule *****

Due / Starting		Amount
59	12-30-09	950.00
1	11-30-14	950.00

DMV fees	275.00
Insurance premiums	.00
Total purchase	37,060.78

Amount financed	37,060.78
APR	17.9
Finance charges	19,938.22
Total of payments	57,000.00
Total sales price	57,000.00

Trade-in	.00
Less payoff	.00
Net trade-in	.00
Deferred down	.00
Amount paid now	.00
Total down payment	.00

Price	35,796.85
Accessories	.00
Doc fee	35.00
Dealer smog	.00
Sales tax	2,956.12
Service agreement	.00
Cash price	38,787.97
DMV fees	287.00
Insurance premiums	.00
Total purchase	39,074.97
Trade-in	.00
Less payoff	.00
Net trade-in	.00
Deferred down	.00
Amount paid now	.00
Total down payment	.00

***** Payment Schedule *****

Due / Starting		Amount
59	12-30-09	1,000.00
1	11-30-14	1,000.00

Amount financed	39,074.97
APR	17.9
Finance charges	20,925.03
Total of payments	60,000.00
Total sales price	60,000.00

We saved extra money on our monthly payment for our minivan.
We have just started our new family. This book, *Buyers vs. Liars*, is
a great book for every family.

This boat retail price was listed at $150,000, and he did not negotiate. He paid full price with $75,000 down.

Price	150,000.00
Accessories	395.00
Doc fee	35.00
Dealer smog	29.00
Sales tax	12,412.87
Service agreement	1,695.00
Cash price	164,566.87

DMV fees	246.00
Insurance premiums	.00
Total purchase	164,812.87

Trade-in	.00
Less payoff	.00
Net trade-in	.00
Deferred down	.00
Amount paid now	75,000.00
Total down payment	75,000.00

***** Payment Schedule *****

Due / Starting		Amount
83	12-30-09	1,967.46
1	11-30-16	1,967.46

Amount financed	89,812.87
APR	19.00
Finance charges	75,447.77
Total of payments	165.266.64
Total sales price	240,266.64

Payment Schedule Chart at 19.9% at 60 Months

Price	6,731.77
Accessories	.00
Doc fee	35.00
Dealer smog	.00
Sales tax	558.25
Service agreement	.00
Cash price	7,325.02

***** Payment Schedule *****

Due / Starting		Amount
59	12-30-09	200.00
1	11-30-14	200.00

DMV fees	99.00
Insurance premiums	.00
Total purchase	7,440.02

Amount financed	7,440.02
APR	19.9
Finance charges	4,575.98
Total of payments	12,000.00
Total sales price	12,000.00

Trade-in	.00
Less payoff	.00
Net trade-in	.00
Deferred down	.00
Amount paid now	.00
Total down payment	.00

****

Price	8,454.35
Accessories	.00
Doc fee	35.00
Dealer smog	.00
Sales tax	700.37
Service agreement	.00
Cash price	9,189.72

***** Payment Schedule *****

Due / Starting		Amount
59	12-30-09	250.00
1	11-30-14	250.00

DMV fees	110.00
Insurance premiums	.00
Total purchase	9,299.72

Amount financed	9,299.72
APR	19.9
Finance charges	5,700.28
Total of payments	15,000.00
Total sales price	15,000.00

Trade-in	.00
Less payoff	.00
Net trade-in	.00
Deferred down	.00
Amount paid now	.00
Total down payment	.00

Price	10,231.89
Accessories	.00
Doc fee	35.00
Dealer smog	.00
Sales tax	847.01
Service agreement	.00
Cash price	11,113.90

DMV fees	121.00
Insurance premiums	.00
Total purchase	11,234.90

Trade-in	.00
Less payoff	.00
Net trade-in	.00
Deferred down	.00
Amount paid now	.00
Total down payment	.00

***** Payment Schedule *****

	Due / Starting	Amount
59	12-30-09	300.00
1	11-30-14	300.00

Amount financed	11,234.90
APR	19.9
Finance charges	6,765.10
Total of payments	18,000.00
Total sales price	18,000.00

****

Price	11,899.42
Accessories	.00
Doc fee	35.00
Dealer smog	.00
Sales tax	984.58
Service agreement	.00
Cash price	12,919.00

DMV fees	132.00
Insurance premiums	.00
Total purchase	13,051.00

Trade-in	.00
Less payoff	.00
Net trade-in	.00
Deferred down	.00
Amount paid now	.00
Total down payment	.00

***** Payment Schedule *****

	Due / Starting	Amount
59	12-30-09	350.00
1	11-30-14	350.00

Amount financed	13,051.00
APR	19.9
Finance charges	7,949.00
Total of payments	21,000.00
Total sales price	21,000.00

Price	13,621.04
Accessories	.00
Doc fee	35.00
Dealer smog	.00
Sales tax	1,126.62
Service agreement	.00
Cash price	14,782.66

DMV fees	144.00
Insurance premiums	.00
Total purchase	14,926.66

Trade-in	.00
Less payoff	.00
Net trade-in	.00
Deferred down	.00
Amount paid now	.00
Total down payment	.00

***** Payment Schedule *****

Due / Starting		Amount
59	12-30-09	400.00
1	11-30-14	400.00

Amount financed	14,926.66
APR	19.9
Finance charges	9,073.34
Total of payments	24,000.00
Total sales price	24,000.00

****

Price	15,344.55
Accessories	.00
Doc fee	35.00
Dealer smog	.00
Sales tax	1,268.81
Service agreement	.00
Cash price	16,648.36

DMV fees	154.00
Insurance premiums	.00
Total purchase	16,802.36

Trade-in	.00
Less payoff	.00
Net trade-in	.00
Deferred down	.00
Amount paid now	.00
Total down payment	.00

***** Payment Schedule *****

Due / Starting		Amount
59	12-30-09	450.00
1	11-30-14	450.00

Amount financed	16,802.36
APR	19.9
Finance charges	10,197.64
Total of payments	27,000.00
Total sales price	27,000.00

Price	17,066.16	
Accessories	.00	
Doc fee	35.00	
Dealer smog	.00	
Sales tax	1,410.84	
Service agreement	.00	
Cash price	18,512.00	

***** Payment Schedule *****

Due / Starting		Amount
59	12-30-09	500.00
1	11-30-14	500.00

DMV fees	166.00
Insurance premiums	.00
Total purchase	18,678.00

Amount financed	18,678.00
APR	19.9
Finance charges	11,322.00
Total of payments	30,000.00
Total sales price	30,000.00

Trade-in	.00
Less payoff	.00
Net trade-in	.00
Deferred down	.00
Amount paid now	.00
Total down payment	.00

****

Price	18,788.65
Accessories	.00
Doc fee	35.00
Dealer smog	.00
Sales tax	1,552.95
Service agreement	.00
Cash price	20,376.66

***** Payment Schedule *****

Due / Starting		Amount
59	12-30-09	550.00
1	11-30-14	550.00

DMV fees	177.00
Insurance premiums	.00
Total purchase	20,553.60

Amount financed	20,553.60
APR	19.9
Finance charges	12,446.40
Total of payments	33,000.00
Total sales price	33,000.00

Trade-in	.00
Less payoff	.00
Net trade-in	.00
Deferred down	.00
Amount paid now	.00
Total down payment	.00

Price	20,511.18	
Accessories	.00	
Doc fee	35.00	
Dealer smog	.00	
Sales tax	1,695.05	
Service agreement	.00	
Cash price	22,241.23	

***** Payment Schedule *****

Due / Starting		Amount
59	12-30-09	600.00
1	11-30-14	600.00

DMV fees	188.00
Insurance premiums	.00
Total purchase	22,429.23

Amount financed	22,429.23
APR	19.9
Finance charges	13,570.77
Total of payments	36,000.00
Total sales price	36,000.00

Trade-in	.00
Less payoff	.00
Net trade-in	.00
Deferred down	.00
Amount paid now	.00
Total down payment	.00

****

Price	22,232.86
Accessories	.00
Doc fee	35.00
Dealer smog	.00
Sales tax	1,837.09
Service agreement	.00
Cash price	24,104.95

***** Payment Schedule *****

Due / Starting		Amount
59	12-30-09	650.00
1	11-30-14	650.00

DMV fees	200.00
Insurance premiums	.00
Total purchase	24,304.95

Amount financed	24,304.95
APR	19.9
Finance charges	14,895.05
Total of payments	39,000.00
Total sales price	39,000.00

Trade-in	.00
Less payoff	.00
Net trade-in	.00
Deferred down	.00
Amount paid now	.00
Total down payment	.00

		***** Payment Schedule *****	
Price	23,956.25		
Accessories	.00		
Doc fee	35.00	Due / Starting	Amount
Dealer smog	.00		
Sales tax	1,979.27		
Service agreement	.00	59 12-30-09	700.00
Cash price	25,970.52	1 11-30-14	700.00
DMV fees	210.00	Amount financed	25,180.52
Insurance premiums	.00	APR	19.9
Total purchase	26,180.52	Finance charges	15,819.48
		Total of payments	42,000.00
		Total sales price	42,000.00
Trade-in	.00		
Less payoff	.00		
Net trade-in	.00		
Deferred down	.00		
Amount paid now	.00		
Total down payment	.00		

****

		***** Payment Schedule *****	
Price	25,677.87		
Accessories	.00		
Doc fee	35.00	Due / Starting	Amount
Dealer smog	.00		
Sales tax	2,121.31		
Service agreement	.00	59 12-30-09	750.00
Cash price	27,834.18	1 11-30-14	750.00
DMV fees	222.00	Amount financed	28,056.18
Insurance premiums	.00	APR	19.9
Total purchase	28,056.18	Finance charges	16,943.82
		Total of payments	45,000.00
		Total sales price	45,000.00
Trade-in	.00		
Less payoff	.00		
Net trade-in	.00		
Deferred down	.00		
Amount paid now	.00		
Total down payment	.00		

		***** Payment Schedule *****	
Price	27,399.41		
Accessories	.00		
Doc fee	35.00	Due / Starting	Amount
Dealer smog	.00		
Sales tax	2,263.33		
Service agreement	.00	59 12-30-09	800.00
Cash price	29,697.74	1 11-30-14	800.00
DMV fees	232.00	Amount financed	29,929.74
Insurance premiums	.00	APR	19.9
Total purchase	29,929.74	Finance charges	18,070.26
		Total of payments	48,000.00
		Total sales price	48,000.00
Trade-in	.00		
Less payoff	.00		
Net trade-in	.00		
Deferred down	.00		
Amount paid now	.00		
Total down payment	.00		

****

		***** Payment Schedule *****	
Price	29,155.56		
Accessories	.00		
Doc fee	35.00	Due / Starting	Amount
Dealer smog	.00		
Sales tax	2,408.22		
Service agreement	.00	59 12-30-09	850.00
Cash price	31,598.78	1 11-30-14	850.00
DMV fees	244.00	Amount financed	31,842.78
Insurance premiums	.00	APR	19.9
Total purchase	31,842.78	Finance charges	19,157.22
		Total of payments	51,000.00
		Total sales price	51,000.00
Trade-in	.00		
Less payoff	.00		
Net trade-in	.00		
Deferred down	.00		
Amount paid now	.00		
Total down payment	.00		

Price	30,877.13
Accessories	.00
Doc fee	35.00
Dealer smog	.00
Sales tax	2,550.25
Service agreement	.00
Cash price	33,462.38

***** Payment Schedule *****

Due / Starting		Amount
59	12-30-09	900.00
1	11-30-14	900.00

DMV fees	256.00
Insurance premiums	.00
Total purchase	33,718.38

Amount financed	33,718.38
APR	19.9
Finance charges	20,281.62
Total of payments	54,000.00
Total sales price	54,000.00

Trade-in	.00
Less payoff	.00
Net trade-in	.00
Deferred down	.00
Amount paid now	.00
Total down payment	.00

****

Price	32,598.67
Accessories	.00
Doc fee	35.00
Dealer smog	.00
Sales tax	2,692.27
Service agreement	.00
Cash price	35,325.94

***** Payment Schedule *****

Due / Starting		Amount
59	12-30-09	950.00
1	11-30-14	950.00

DMV fees	266.00
Insurance premiums	.00
Total purchase	35,591.94

Amount financed	35,591.94
APR	19.9
Finance charges	21,408.06
Total of payments	57,000.00
Total sales price	57,000.00

Trade-in	.00
Less payoff	.00
Net trade-in	.00
Deferred down	.00
Amount paid now	.00
Total down payment	.00

Price	34,320.20
Accessories	.00
Doc fee	35.00
Dealer smog	.00
Sales tax	2,834.30
Service agreement	.00
Cash price	37,189.50
DMV fees	266.00
Insurance premiums	.00
Total purchase	37,455.50
Trade-in	.00
Less payoff	.00
Net trade-in	.00
Deferred down	.00
Amount paid now	.00
Total down payment	.00

***** Payment Schedule *****

Due / Starting		Amount
59	12-30-09	1,000.00
1	11-30-14	1,000.00

Amount financed	37,455.50
APR	19.9
Finance charges	22,554.50
Total of payments	60,000.00
Total sales price	60,000.00

The Secrets of the Auto Dealerships Are Out!

People need to know this information because the "rich people are too greedy and don't really care about the citizens." Every house should have a copy of *Buyers vs. Liars: Secrets of the Auto Dealership*. It will save us billions of dollars. Our families need help saving money daily.

WHEN A CUSTOMER WANTS TO PURCHASE A VEHICLE FROM THE LOCAL NEWSPAPER, REMEMBER THERE ARE SOME PEOPLE WHO WANT TO ROB YOU FOR YOUR MONEY.

DON'T TRUST THEM! MEET THEM IN THE DAYTIME SOMEWHERE SAFE, AND REMEMBER, SOME OF THEM JUST WANT YOUR CASH FOR FREE.

**NOW IF
YOU DON'T
WANT
TO FINANCE
ANY VEHICLES,**

YOU CAN JUST . . .

. . . . **RIDE A BIKE**

Stephanie Hengst is yelling from the hilltop . . . on Mt. Tamalpais, CA.

"The secret is out!"

The United Kingdom and Canada Are Down with
Buyers vs. Liars!
Are You a Buyer, or Are You a Liar?

Buyers vs. Liars

Decade after decade, the automobile dealers have ripped off millions of consumers for billions of dollars by lying to them and hiding profit in their monthly payments. This book will show you how to keep from getting ripped off by the dealerships, and I will show you exactly how and where they are hiding your hard-earned money without your permission. The *consumers* are the *victims*.

The Secret Is Out

Every day, thousands of customers end up with outrageous monthly payments. They are hidden in their prices, rates, terms, service agreements, payments and sometimes all of the above. There are secrets on how to keep thousands of dollars from ever leaving your hands. Here is the solution on how to save money without getting ripped off. By following the *Buyers vs. Liars* information guide for your next new/used, hybrid or electric vehicle in America, you will know the TRUTH!

"PROTECT YOUR MONEY" FROM THESE "DISHONEST DEALERS"
"Fight for the Price."

Glossary

ACCESSORIES: EXTRA OPTIONAL equipment added to the vehicle or to enhance performance.

ACV: The "actual cash value" is what the vehicle is actually worth.

APR: The "annual percentage rate" is the amount of finance charge that is paid per year on the money that is borrowed against the loan.

Bad credit: A customer who has had problems making monthly payments on schedule, due to late payments, slow payments, divorce, illness, or even bankruptcy.

Co-signer: A family member who signs his name on the contract to assist the original buyer in funding the vehicle. The co-signer is responsible for the monthly payments throughout the contract, or their credit can be in jeopardy.

Credit rating: A member's credit scores that determine a customer's APR.

Credit union: A cooperative lending and saving association that makes a loan to its member.

Down payment: A certain amount of money used to lower the customer's monthly payment. These payments are sometimes in the form of cash or credit card.

Drive-off fees: When leasing a vehicle, they say "no down," but fees are usually required.

Extended service contract: To coexist with and extend in conjunction with their original service contract. Most of the time, it does not cover some of the simple breakdown parts of their vehicle.

Fees: Extra charges used for paper processing of the vehicle's information.

Hidden charges: Unauthorized charges that are stolen from customers without their approval.

Incentives: The dealership's reasons to sell their vehicle for less because the manufacturer is giving the dealers $1,000.00 incentive to sell a certain selected model. Then the dealers can sell that vehicle model $800.00 less than invoice and still make a $200.00 profit.

Low ball: This is what a dealership will give a customer when they are shopping (dealership versus another dealership). The low-ball price is so low that it will make the customer come back to the dealers.

Over allowance: An over allowance is what dealerships give customers to help them out of their trade. The dealership still earns a profit.

Paper trip: When the dealership has the customer sign all documents before leaving the dealership (they must get approval from the bank first). The customer's credit is uncertain.

Pick-up payments: When a customer does not have all of his down payment, the dealership will give them more time to gather additional funds to complete their contract. Normally it is two weeks later.

Repo: Repossession is when the lending institution reclaims property back from the customer who failed to keep his payment arrangement.

Roach: The customer's credit is so bad that they can't finance anything even with a co-signer—they will even check their cash.